Laugh and Live

Laugh and Live
Reclaiming Our Sense of Humor

Linda Hutchinson
and a Dozen Others

To Sally —
Wishing you many laughs
& a light ♡,
Linda H — ha!
4/1/04

North Star Press of St. Cloud, Inc.

Cover photo: Barbara La Valleur

Cover design: Seal Dwyer

Artwork on back cover photo: Andrea La Valleur-Purvis

Copyright © 2004 Linda Hutchinson
www.haha-team.com

ISBN: 0-87839-204-1

First edition, April 1, 2004

Printed in the United States of America
by Versa Press, Inc.

Published by
North Star Press of St. Cloud, Inc.
P.O. Box 451
St. Cloud, Minnesota 56302
nspress@cloudnet.com

Dedication

To my mother, Mary, a warm, wise, witty woman;
to the Sisters of Saint Benedict in St. Joseph, Minnesota,
a community of warm, wise, witty women;
to my son, Jesse, a warm, witty, wise guy.
Three of my favorite sources of humor.

And to the laughers of the world.

Acknowledgements

The Baker's Dozen who made the biggest difference:

the Studium, the program of the Sisters of St. Benedict that made the research and writing of this book possible;

Vicki Gee-Treft, grandmother of four, five with this book;

Norma Dickau, for laughter and chocolate;

Consultants: S. Nancy Hynes, O.S.B., for laughter and believing in me; Sheila Rausch, O.S.B., for being fun and funny; and JoAnn Shroyer, for being joyful;

Editors: Barbara La Valleur, for generosity; Julie Berg, for courage; and Corinne Dwyer, for patience;

Cover design by Seal Dwyer, for her creativity and technical skills;

Eustolio Benavides III for inspiration, Paul Halvorson for invaluable constructive criticism; and

My family, for being fun and funny, especially my sister, Joyce, who prayed for a little sister and got me, although she doesn't always consider me to be an answer from heaven;

Others who made a significant difference, sharing time and expertise:

Anahata Morris, Andrea La Valleur-Purvis, Annie Heymans, Betsy Mahowald, Carissa Renkin, Heather Charette, Jan Bucher, Jane Dawson, Jeanie Wilkens, Jerry Hoistad, Jill Schwimmer, S. Joan Schmidt, O.P., JoAnn Koraleski, Joel Goodman and The Humor Project, Judith Hanks, Julie Larson, Landmark Education, the library staff at the College of St. Benedict, Linda Wimmer, Liz Dwyer, Margaret Johnson, Merrilyn Belgum, Polly Jeneva, Rebecca Miller, Steve Wilson and The World Laughter Tour, and the following sisters at the St. Benedict Monastery: S. Adelyne Imperatore, S. Clara Antony, S. Cynthia Schmitt, S. Dolores Super, S.

My dear friends who gave a Saturday morning, laughed for an hour straight and didn't make the book cover.   Barbara La Valleur

Ingrid Anderson, S. Janelle Sietsema, S. Johanna Becker, S. Kathleen Kalinowski, S. Laurent Trombley, S. Linda Kulzer, S. Louise Koltes, S. Mariterese Woida, S. Marold Kornovich, S. Mary Schneider, S. Merle Nolde, S. Olivia Forster, S. Renee Domeier, S. Rosemary Hoschette, S. Stefanie Weisgram, S. Suzanne Helmin, and S. Thomasette Scheeler;

And unknown authors who generated humorous stories and quotes and didn't get credit for their creativity.

The people who participated in my educational programs for all I learned with you.

Contents

Introduction

What if the hokey pokey really is what it's all about?

—Author unknown

People often ask me when I got started in the humor business. I say: "Fourth grade." As I recall, during fourth grade the sharing and telling time was particularly good. So good, that I took the stories home and shared them with my family around the supper table. It was a great source of positive attention. I continue to strive for positive attention through humor.

Although I do have many good stories to share, I don't pretend to be a comedian. I am a humor educator. When people looking for a comedian call me, I refer them to Merrilyn Belgum and Susan Vass.

Merrilyn once spoke in front of 2,000 women in Milwaukee. She returned to Minneapolis and reported that she got a "standing ovulation." By the way, she brings seventy-eight years of experience to her comedy. Used with permission

My favorite example of Susan's humor is about taking her ninety-year-old friend Agnes shopping. Agnes was usually pretty upbeat, but one day she was depressed. Susan asked her what was wrong. Agnes said that her husband and she had decided to get a divorce. Susan exclaimed, "After seventy years of marriage,

1

you're going to get a divorce now?" Agnes said, "We thought we'd wait until the children were dead." Used with permission

I am a middle-class, middle-aged Midwesterner of German and Irish heritage, a mother, farmers' daughter, sister, aunt, friend, entrepreneur, heterosexual, feminist, radical, peace and justice advocate, ecumenical Christian, and world citizen. I am a student and teacher of humor, and I am certified to lead Laughter Clubs. These "handles" influence how I see the world, how I see humor, what I consider valuable to share.

My son knows that I am three-quarters German and his dad is three-quarters German. He decided that he must be six-quarters German.

Me and my brother, Dave, with our pet pig, Porkchop Family photo

Introduction

I mentioned being a feminist. Because there is a lot of misunderstanding about what it means to be a feminist, I want to explain what it means to me. Feminism includes 1) exploration and validation of all aspects of women's experience, 2) recovery of women's history, 3) affirmation of women's leadership, 4) insistence on full collaboration with men, 5) resistance to the unique ways poverty affects women and children, 6) refusal to deny the fact or the scope of sexual abuse or harassment, and 7) vigilance against the fear and ignorance that generate a backlash against claims to share equally with men (adapted from a list by Joann Wolski Conn).

Since 1993, I have owned and operated a business, Hutchinson Associates, *ha!* in which I design and deliver educational programs for corporations, non-profit organizations, educational institutions and professional associations. (For more information, go to: www.haha-team.com.)

Just as I design my training programs to be practical, pithy and playful, that is also my intention for this book. I hope, as you read this, that you are affirmed in what you already know and do with laughter and humor, that you get new ideas and insights to actually use . . . and that you get several laughs!

From *Ma, can I be a feminist and still like men?* by Nicole Hollander   Used with permission

3

With regard to the playful part (in bold), there are different jokes for different folks. In fact, I have included a variety of types of humor beyond jokes—stories, cartoons, photographs, word play and some funny quotes. According to Dr. Robert Provine, University of Maryland, only ten percent of laughter is from jokes. My challenge in putting this book together was to find various ways to reflect the other ninety percent of sources of laughter. Since we have a tendency to reduce humor to jokes, my commitment is to demonstrate that there is more to humor than jokes. In conversation, when I bring up the word "humor," people often immediately think "jokes." I distinguish between stories and jokes: stories connect with the rest of the content of a conversation; they don't interrupt the flow. Jokes often interrupt a conversation. Jokes are often about cleverness and self-presentation.

There are numerous types of humor and various descriptive words for humor: absurdity, sarcasm, slapstick, puns and other forms of word play, satire, jokes, stories, pranks, teasing, silliness, corniness, wit, food art, comedy, jests, exaggeration, jocularity, incongruity, nonsense, riddles, juxtaposition, tickling, vulgarity, and ludicrousness.

As human beings we have a tendency to think that others should laugh at the same things we do. We don't often consider the idea that what we find funny is based in our individual life experiences.

For example, there is a joke in the deaf community about two people out for a walk, one is hearing-impaired, and the other is not. They notice the birds on a telephone wire. One bird jumps up and seems to sign the letter T, another does the same thing, and still another seems to sign the letter Y. The hearing-impaired person says, "Oh, that's a TTY line."

by Corinne Dwyer

4

In order to "get the joke," you need to have some familiarity with the hearing-impaired culture. TTY is the name of the telephone service for people who have a hearing impairment.

We have a tendency to think others should laugh at or be offended by the same things we are. People are funny about humor in that way. We don't expect others to enjoy the same movies, or music, or poetry. We like it if they do, but I don't think we have the same expectations of sharing these personal tastes as we do with humor. Feel free to differ with me and to let me know.

The practical part is the ideas section of each chapter. In the interest of being practical, before you read further, I urge you to identify an area in your life that you are taking too seriously. It could be a particular relationship at home or at work, or it could be your lack of relationships. It could be parenting, a stressful project at work, finances, or a prickly family member. For me, technology causes me to lose my humor. I continually need to call forth my funny bone. As you read this book, keep in mind an area you would like to lighten up. Listen for ways humor can influence that area of your life.

After I shared my frustration with technology and my need to maintain my sense of humor, especially with regard to computer problems, my friend Vicki sent the following:

Serene Japanese Computer Messages:

- **The Web site you seek cannot be located, but countless more exist.**
- **Chaos reigns within. Reflect, repent and reboot. Order shall return.**
- **Yesterday it worked. Today it is not working. Windows is like that.**
- **Stay the patient course. Of little worth is your ire. The network is down.**
- **A crash reduces your expensive computer to a simple stone.**
- **Three things are certain: death, taxes, and lost data. Guess which has occurred?**
- **Having been erased, the document you are seeking must now be retyped.**
- **Serious error, all shortcuts have disappeared.**
- **Screen. Mind. Both are blank.** On over 8,000 Web sites

Another area of life where I tend to lose my humor is around money. I discovered a book that helped me lighten up, *The Soul of Money* by Lynne Twist. Although not a humorous book, it is one of the most powerful books I have ever read. There are ways to lighten up without laughter. By examining my attitudes toward money, I was able to replace my fears with freedom and a sense of purpose. Twist shows how to live consciously in relationship to money and by doing so to transform all areas of life.

> *A lot of money is tainted.*
>
> *It taint yours and it taint mine.*
>
> Author unknown

If we don't laugh at people's jokes, we are often accused of not having a sense of humor. We all have a sense of humor. The question is how to further develop it. I continually challenge myself to expand my humor in new ways—playing with props, consciously looking for humor in everyday life and, more recently, allowing myself to be more spontaneous instead of censoring myself.

Most of us were taught not to talk with strangers, which is critical to our safety as children and wise to practice as adults as well, but not all the time. Perhaps we have taken the lesson to an extreme. While shopping one day, I saw a man delivering an abundance of flower bouquets. I said to him, "For me?" He said, "I love you!" His witty response made my day, even if the flowers weren't for me.

With regard to being pithy, which means substantive, my intention is to nourish you with food for thought that is highly readable and not overly academic. There is an abundance of academic treatises on humor. (See bibliography.) I invite you to think of this book as a conversation—a one-sided conversation, as I get to do all the talking. I do, however, invite your response.

Defining Humor

> Dorothy Parker wrote, "I thought, on starting this composition . . . that I should define what humor means to me. However, every time I tried to, I had to go and lie down with a cold wet cloth on my head."
>
> —Gloria Kaufman,
> *In Stitches: A Patchwork of Feminist Humor and Satire*

Defining humor can be difficult. For me, humor is about attitude, about our *take* on life. It is much more about being lighthearted than it is about being glib with jokes. It is about seeing and enjoying the incongruities in life.

Supposedly, our sense of humor is one thing that sets humans apart from other animals. As far as we know, sheep do not have a sense of humor. I don't think camels do either. Come to think of it, any animal that spits might have a sense of humor. Many animals—ferrets, goat kids, dolphins, chimpanzees—have a sense of play and some even seem to laugh, but having a sense of humor may be a privilege of human beings. I might be wrong though. Maybe some lighthearted elephants or pigeons are out there telling "people" jokes.

Visit Dharma and friends at www.DharmaTheCat.com. Winner of the 10 Best on the Web Award.   Used with permission

The words "humor" and "humility" have the same root—the ancient Indo-European *ghom*, best translated as the English "humus," which means "of the earth." No wonder I like earthy humor.

The last chapter explores the relationship between humor and humility and being human. In fact, after I had compiled a list of over 110 ideas for giving and receiving humor, I realized that the key to humor is humility. The 111th idea is to pray for humility.

Humor is a word of many meanings, some very personal. What does it mean to you? Identify the words you associate with humor. Ask others what it means to them. It makes for a great conversation. Notice if it turns into a joke-telling session.

As human beings, we are meaning-makers. What would happen if we consciously chose to look for humorous meanings to interpret the events in life? Sometimes the funny interpretations just happen; many times they don't. Look for the comedy within the dramas of your life, especially when being "deadly serious." Consider the difference between deadly seriousness and lively lightness.

This book is not the last word on humor. Humor may always remain somewhat of a mystery. The more I delve into its meaning, the more wonderfully mysterious it is.

The first chapter of this book briefly explores some barriers to humor. I introduce the idea of identifying your personal humor heritage, the myths and messages in your life that encourage or discourage humor development. As I wrote my own humor story, I noted that my concern for being feminine was a barrier to developing my sense of humor.

In the chapter on humor in personal relationships, I briefly explore humor and gender. What are some differences between women's and men's humor? How can humor be a tool for bringing both closer together? This is only a beginning exploration. A whole book could be written on this topic alone. For that matter, each chapter of this book could be a book and in some cases is, for example, *The Healing Power of Humor* and *Humor at Work*.

Major themes of this book are humor in relationships, learning and creativity, healing and stress. I choose not to elaborate on the healing power of humor since that topic has already been covered. (See bibliography.) However, as a certified Laughter Club leader, I write about the most exciting new development—Laughter Clubs. After reading the chapter on learning and creativity, I urge you to use humor in learning new things whether developing technical skills or expanding your knowledge.

Five chapters are devoted to humor in relationships. In my research and reflection, I discovered that relational trust is a key to giving and receiving healthy humor. I focus on relational trust between men and women, within families and the workplace, as well as across cultures, and even in our relationship with our version of God or a Higher Being.

Besides gender, the other two areas of humor that are most exciting to me are culture and spirituality. My two colleagues, Eustolio Benavides III and Vicki Gee-Treft, and I are committed to expanding these topics, developing a series of articles for the next book. (Send us your questions and suggestions.) Rather than have a separate chapter on diversity, I incorporated illustrations of humor and diversity and community throughout the book.

I also chose to focus on the positive power of humor rather than dwell on offensive humor. In *Punchlines*, which deals with the violence of American humor, William Keough calls attention to the way our language uses such phrases as "punch lines," "knock 'em dead," and "kill the audience." I will use the phrase "laugh line" instead of "punch line." Several articles on humor harassment in the workplace are also available on the Web.

What I have learned about who we are as human, humorous beings is:

- We all want to belong.
- We all want to contribute.
- We all want to laugh, play and have fun.
- We all want to love and be loved.

Humor makes a difference for better and for worse in all these areas! Let's be pro-active and fill the world with the positive power of humor.

Key:

playful - bold
practical - shaded
pithy - regular type

I

Humor Heritage

Why We Don't Have an Abundance of Humor

Given all the benefits of humor—enhancing relationships; building self-esteem; promoting well-being of body, mind, and spirit; inspiring creativity; reducing stress; and encouraging learning—why don't all of us have an abundance of healthy humor in our lives? Actually, there may be many reasons, most rooted in fear. Our apprehensions have the ability to paralyze our funny bone. Strangely, it takes courage to risk adding humor to life. At the same time, it is ironic to note that humor has the ability to transform fear. Do you see a cycle here? Underneath it all, I believe the problem is a fear of losing control. What would happen if we laughed so hard we lost control, cried or, worse yet, wet our pants?

As mentioned earlier, we've reduced humor to joke-telling, which many of us think we can't do to save our lives. Often this is a self-fulfilling prophecy. We fear that we will forget the "laugh line," and then, of course, we do.

Another fear is that we won't get the joke, that the funny part will slip over our heads or under our horizons or that, somehow, it will make us feel silly or stupid. Our fear gets in the way of getting it. Sometimes we allow others to tell us we can't tell jokes or that we don't have a sense of humor, and we begin to believe that. The fact is that we all have a sense of humor; it's just that some of us have received more encouragement to develop it than others have. Thankfully, there's no time limit on its development, no specific age by which it must be developed. Come to think of it, there is a time limit. We probably want to have developed it before we're dead.

Myths about humor abound, most of these negative. Some of these myths can inhibit our ability to give and receive healthy humor. For example, laughter in the work setting is out of place and it's unprofessional to be funny at work. We equate seriousness with getting the job done. We fear that we will get into trouble. (That is a possibility because the myth exists throughout the hierarchy of business. Our boss might also think it's inappropriate or unprofessional.) We think people won't like us or that we might offend them with our humor. A male friend stopped telling jokes just on the off chance he might offend someone.

Another myth is that laughter and learning don't go together. Teachers fear they might lose control of the classroom. Some of us learned that laughter in church is out of place. Or that laughter during times of grief is inappropriate. As you read about my humor heritage below, you will hear how the societal message—that it is unfeminine to be funny—impaired my humor development.

Some of us had a deprived childhood. We grew up in a "too-serious" family. We think it is too late to develop our funny bone. Fortunately that's also a myth and far from true. Many of us were told at one time or another to "Grow up!" "Wipe that silly grin off your face!" or "Act your age!"

Few of us reached adulthood without an experience of people laughing at us when we didn't think they should. My son prepared a magic trick for his kindergarten class. If it had been only his classmates, all probably would have been okay. But the parents were there. He was so darn cute and funny while performing his magic trick that the grown-ups laughed. He was embarrassed. That can be the kind of experience in which we decide, "I will never do anything like that again." He got a laugh when he was being serious and wanted to be taken seriously. (I asked my son about this experience; fortunately it did not have a lasting, profound effect on him.)

I would assert that most, if not all, of us have had at least one bad experience when people laughed when we didn't want them to, or we wanted people to laugh and they didn't.

I introduce the concept of humor heritage—our humor inheritance—the messages and meanings we attach to previous experiences.

Whether we had a deprived childhood or not, we have all had experiences that either encouraged or impaired the development of our sense of humor. These can be small setbacks, where we decide not to be funny in a specific situation or in front of specific people. Or they can be negative, and we decide to give up.

My intention in this section is to increase consciousness of our humor heritage. Let us claim the empowering messages and discard the messages that were not. As I share stories about my family, church, and school—the institutions that shaped my early life—I invite you to reflect on the meanings and messages of your own early experiences within your family, church, synagogue, mosque, and educational institutions. Besides considering the influence of major institutions on your early life, another approach is to explore your personal humor heritage chronologically. I will do both.

My Humor Heritage—Family

I was raised in a fun-loving, funny family. Though we were not perfect, laughter and play were present in our home and still are when we get together. As mentioned earlier, I got my start in this business as a result of the encouraging responses I received from sharing stories around the supper table.

In terms of my parents, Dad was the funny one; Mom the serious, responsible one. This is how I remember them. As I mention this to others, more often than not, they agree that their fathers were also funnier than their mothers. We didn't realize how humorous Mom was until after Dad died. This was more than a situation where we just didn't notice our mother's humor. Somehow, her own humor heritage had suppressed it. Women often have more freedom and confidence to be funny as they get older.

Whether a blessing or a curse, I do seem to remember jokes. Is that because I grew up in a predominantly male family? Joke telling seems to be more popular among men.

Teasing is another predominantly male form of humor. One of my childhood memories is of being teased by my older brother. He teased me until I cried, then tickled me to make me laugh so he

Dad had this photo taken on his honeymoon. One might think it isn't humorous risking one's life—Dad was no cowboy. What if he was thrown and trampled right in front of his new bride? The photo gets a whole lot funnier when it's known that the horse was stuffed.

My wise, witty mom   Photo by Barbara La Valleur

wouldn't get into trouble. Older siblings tend to tease younger ones more. This is particularly true in the case of older brothers teasing younger sisters. I wonder whether that is where the "battle of the sexes" begins.

Humor Heritage—Church

One of my earliest memories is being carried out of church at age five. I have no idea what I said or did to warrant this action. It became clear to me, however, that church was serious business. We certainly were not allowed to laugh in church unless the priest cracked a joke, and most of those weren't particularly funny to children. I assert that the majority of church-going people have experiences of suppressing laughter in church.

Recently, I heard a story about a little boy who was carried out of church. His parents did everything to get him to settle down and pay attention, to no avail. Finally, the Dad picked the little boy up and headed for the door. Just as he was going out the door, the little fellow hollered, "Pray for me, pray for me."

It is no coincidence that I teach college courses and lead retreats on the relationship between humor and spirituality.

When I was memorizing the Lord's Prayer, we had a priest named Father Daly. While learning "give us this day our daily bread," I thought we were supposed to give Father Daly our bread.

Another early church memory took place while visiting a cousin in Iowa when I was seven years old. We were waiting in line to go to confession. I don't know what they fed us for supper, but we both had bad cases of flatulence. (Now isn't that a funny word?) The more we giggled, the more we farted. There is nothing quite like breaking two "rules" at once while waiting in line for confession to report our sins. I am grateful to this day that it happened in her home town and not mine. I like to say I left her in her own pew.

Humor Heritage—School

Apart from the fun of recess and sharing time, most of what I remember about laughter and play in elementary school in the late 1950s was getting into trouble. In fifth grade I was sent to the cloak room for laughing when Peter Cole made a "funny face" at me. I don't think he received any punishment, and his "funny face" didn't stay that way.

Finding one of her students making faces at others, Ms. Smith stopped to gently reprove the child. Smiling sweetly, the Sunday School teacher said, "Bobby, when I was a child I was told that if I made ugly faces, it would freeze and I would stay like that." Bobby looked up and innocently replied, "Well, Ms. Smith, you can't say you weren't warned." On 93 Web sites

Again, it is no coincidence that I have spent part of my life promoting the idea that learning can be fun; in fact, humor is a great way to open the mind to learning.

Decades in My Humor Heritage

During my adolescence, I became more serious. Customarily, this stage of life is awkward and confusing; it definitely was for me. Although I never did anything bad, I knew sex was serious.

It was critical for me to figure out what it meant to be feminine. I was preoccupied with the idea. Somehow I knew that being funny and feminine did not go together. (See "Humor and Gender") At the time, I had a hard time with my farm heritage. I wanted to be a "town kid."

It was not cool to be from the farm near Hayfield, Minnesota. Today when people ask me where Hayfield is located, I tell them. It is eleven miles from Blooming Prairie, thirty miles from Grand Meadow and a thousand miles from Toadsuck, Arkansas. While growing up, we said we were from near Rochester. I give that bucolic list of places as a way of reclaiming my heritage.

During the late 1960s, life was even more serious. I was in college. I was out to "save" the world. It was easier to look at what was wrong with the world than to deal with the stuff going on within myself. It was an exciting time, and my concern with being feminine was still a big issue. A male friend told me that being a social change activist was unfeminine. He also told me that my nickname, "Hutch," was unfeminine.

A fond memory from this time involved reading bloopers from church bulletins. During my senior year in college, I lived in a commune in Avon, Minnesota, and when guests came to dinner, my housemates would invariably invite me to read the bloopers. I could not read them without getting the giggles. They laughed at my laughing more than at the bloopers.

Church Bulletin Bloopers

- **The ladies of the church have cast off clothing of every kind, and they can be seen in the church basement Friday afternoon.**
- **This afternoon there will be a meeting in the south and north ends of the church. Children will be baptized at both ends.**
- **For those of you who have children and don't know it, we have a nursery downstairs.**

During the 1970s, my twenties, I moved to the big city of Minneapolis, and within a few months I landed the perfect job. Actually, I designed my own job description as the first paid coordinator of the Education Exploration Center, a non-profit Upper Midwest regional resource center for promoting innovations in education. I loved my work and put in long hours organizing conferences and publishing newsletters.

My best friend at the time was better at balancing work and play than I was. Besides her day job, Judy tap-danced for the fun of it. She also participated in the local puppet theater. I didn't have time for such frivolities, but I was devastated when Judy told me that I was too intense. I knew she was right but didn't know how to stop working hard nor how to lighten up.

During the 1980s, I was in my thirties and married. I began to deal with my "stuff." Sometimes, there is nothing like marriage to bring out the best and the worst in us. It might have been more fun had I known about humor therapy.

I appreciated my now ex-husband's humor (and still do). As I reflect on my marriage, I see now that I was jealous of the attention he received for his humor. He is a witty guy, quick with the funny political comments. His is a clever, sophisticated, sometimes sarcastic humor. Mine was much more "low brow" (where does that term come from?). There was a competitive edge to the humor among the men in the couples with whom we hung out. (See photo on page 18.)

My son, Jesse, is one of the joys of my life. We captured his lively, fun, funny presence on paper and audiotape—recording some of the silly things he said and did. I still enjoy listening to the audiotape of Jesse's beautiful young voice and unusual pronunciation of certain words singing "We gonna win!"—the Minnesota Twins baseball team

A group of witty wise guys—sometimes their humor was as "low brow" as mine.   Family photo

theme song. "Strike out a home run; shout a 'hit' hurray." It was 1987, and the Twins won the World Series.

Except for enjoying Jesse, my outlet for humor at the time was not within my home. However, now as a professional education specialist at Hazelden, a world-famous alcohol and drug treatment center, I was encouraged to share my humor in the workplace. Our department designed and facilitated training programs for people from around the world. It was serious business. I found my niche by providing comic relief. At the beginning of workshops and during breaks, I told jokes. When I think of the jokes, I blush. Maybe I shouldn't go public with my humor? Those were the days before my consciousness was raised. My humor included anti-women jokes. I wanted to belong and to receive positive attention in that arena of typical male humor. Usually it worked.

One innocuous joke got big laughs every time and actually turned into a series:

1. **Picture this: I am standing in front of the classroom stiff as a board, arms tight to my side. I ask, "Does anyone know what I represent?" The answer: "The fetal position for the test tube baby."**
2. **Next I ask, "Do you know why babies prefer test tubes?" The answer: "Because they like a womb with a view."**
3. **Then I asked if they know what has red hair, a big nose and grows in a test tube. The answer: Bozo, the clone.**

In the early 1980s people laughed at those jokes. Now they don't produce the same amount of laughter. Timing is critical for humor. In this case, as test tube babies have become a reality, the jokes are not as surprising and could even be considered offensive or insensitive.

One time I told a joke and nobody laughed. While I was facilitating a Hazelden workshop for the World Bank Medical Department, the leader of the workshop, a psychiatrist, encouraged me to tell a Reagan joke. I knew better, but I did it anyway. You could have heard a pin drop. There wasn't even a courtesy grin. I survived, learned from the experience, and consider that instance to be one of my qualifications for being in the humor business. (The joke's not worth repeating.)

Once my consciousness was raised about appropriate and inappropriate humor, I swung in the other direction. For a while, I hesitated to laugh for fear of being politically incorrect. It is important to be conscious of the impact of our humor, especially on those with less power in society. I am no longer hesitant to laugh and am better at distinguishing empowering humor from disempowering humor.

I occasionally make mistakes and appreciate when people are willing to teach me. For example, during a retreat on spirituality and humor, we used the video, *The Search for Signs of Intelligent Life in the Universe*. One participant was offended by the skit about finding a suicide note and also the references to shock treatment. Her courage to speak up enlightened all of us.

My thirties and forties were a time of spiritual exploration. I chose to study theology to explore my religious heritage, and also to search for the answer to my question: What is this spirituality and sexuality thing all about? The search continues. Humor makes the exploration more enjoyable. While I was writing my master's thesis at the College of St. Catherine, St. Paul, Minnesota, on the relationship between spirituality and sexuality, the subject started getting serious. I added cartoons and other amusing illustrations. My professor appreciated the humor breaks while reading the thesis.

Someone asked Mary, the Mother of Jesus, why she always looked so somber in the portraits of her and Baby Jesus. She said, "Well, to tell you the truth, I was hoping for a girl."

Shortly after I began graduate school, my husband and I were divorced. At that time, I also began working at Wilder Forest, a camp and conference center serving non-profit groups. During the five years I worked there, 1987 to 1993, my humor blossomed. The fabulous forest environment and the great people made it a wonderful place to work.

The director of the camp, Jim, set a playful tone and gave us permission to add humor. He had a delightful sense of humor and encouraged my work in humor. One day while Jim was walking across the reception area, carrying a stack of papers, he dropped a couple of pages and then proceeded to drop the others all at once. He was a great one for playing with exaggeration. The education director, Betsy, a great laugher, encouraged us with her laughter. Laughers don't always realize what a great contribution they make. I think if it weren't for the laughers of the world, the funny people wouldn't bother to be funny.

At Wilder Forest, I was free to express my funny self. A few months after my arrival on the job, a couple of us sponsored a Halloween staff party. For the people without costumes (which was ninety-five percent), I offered a hat from my collection of antique women's hats. The hats were used for "dress up" for little kids. They were also a great hit with the grown men. I fondly recall a picture of the maintenance guy wearing a red "Ethel Shreeve" original. Whoever Ethel was, she was pretty classy! (See men in hats on page 18.)

One summer for my own professional development, I attended a five-day humor workshop in the Adirondacks led by Joel and Margie Goodman of The Humor Project (www.humorproject.com). As a result of that experience I was inspired to offer humor workshops at the camp and conference center.

I incorporated the beautiful natural setting into the workshops by giving an extended break time with the assignment of looking for humor in nature. At one point, while deliberating whether to include that assignment, I looked up into a fir tree. There on the branch above me was a beanbag. I considered that my answer.

During the summer, several children's camps used Wilder Forest, and my son spent a couple of weeks at work with me attending day camp. In the middle of the summer, during our own Earth Day activities, the children worked in small groups on various projects like planting a tree or preparing a fruit salad. My son was in the group assigned to form a "nature band" and perform for the other campers. The nature band used mostly items found in the forest to make music: reeds, sticks, pine cones, etc. However, at the performance, my son made another kind of "nature music"—the sounds made when you put your hand under your armpit and squeeze.

Even though I was sad to be laid off from Wilder Forest in 1993, I was able to turn this (apparent) setback into a good thing. I started my own business offering humor workshops and team-building training to corporations, non-profit organizations and associations. This book is a natural progression from that business.

I encourage you to identify the messages and experiences that shaped the development of your humor. Be sure to include the positive experiences.

It's never too late to further develop your sense of humor. And it's never too late to have a happy childhood.

"People ask me, 'Were you funny as a child?' Well, no, I was an accountant."

—Ellen DeGeneres, comedian

Ideas

Besides writing down memories of your own humor heritage, collect the memories of family members. Do this through personal conversations, as well as at family reunions. People remember more when inspired by the stories told by others. Enlist the younger family members to interview the elders. A game called "Family Stories" might also be used to stimulate memories.

Sister Mariterese Woida, O.S.B., made up a family trivia game that prompted many other memories among family members.

After my dad died, I decided to collect a few favorite memories from my sister and five brothers. I included memories of our mother as well, even though she is still living. Their memories were very enlightening, especially since there is a nineteen-year span in age between the oldest and youngest siblings. Their experience of our family is equally different.

My brother David recalled the time Mom was playing cards with us. Something struck her as funny, and she laughed so hard "the tears ran down her leg." At least that's the way he tells it.

My three oldest siblings were rather adventuresome and curious. At one point while in the hay loft, the upper floor of the barn, they decided to see if a cat would land on its feet if dropped to the ground floor. The cat obviously did not want to go it alone and grabbed onto the overalls of the youngest, Jerry, three years old, and took him along. Jerry didn't land on his feet, but he wasn't seriously hurt. All three ran to the house crying. Mom asked, "Who's hurt?" and sent the other two out to play.

In the beginning of this section, I wrote about fear as a barrier to humor. How might we use humor to transform our fears? I was encouraged to learn to dance with my fears, to play with them, to laugh at them. Speaking in public is considered one of the most frightening experiences for most people. It is often suggested that one way to play with the fear of public speaking is to imagine the audience in their underwear.

The most effective means I have found for transforming fear is to identify a commitment larger than the fear. Each time I speak in public, I deal with fear by creating a commitment to the listeners that is bigger than my fear. When I keep that commitment in mind, even if my knees are knocking, I'm able to deliver my message.

I learned about creating a commitment larger than fear through my participation in an educational program called the Landmark Forum. It provides participants with a transformation, a fundamental breakthrough in their ability to relate to life with new freedom and power. This experience made the greatest difference in my giving and receiving humor, including gaining the courage to launch my own business. Check it out at www.landmarkeducation.com.

Play with Props

I use props such as Groucho glasses, supersized glasses, a jester hat, and a button that says IYQ. People read the IYQ button out loud, then I say, "IYQ, too." It either makes them smile or groan; either way works for me.

Caricature by Spikey

Are you a "groan-up?"

It took courage for me to try out props, because for a long time I considered myself "too proper" to use them. Consider wearing Groucho glasses when meeting someone you have never met before at the airport or at a restaurant. It's a great ice-breaker. Recently I heard of a father who wore Groucho glasses the first time he met his daughters' boyfriends. How's that for a family tradition? The young men were initially taken aback, but it didn't take long for them to relax.

Do you have a fun collection?

How about starting a fun collection? My son has the complete collection of Calvin and Hobbes cartoon books. A friend, Sharon, created a fun book of e-mails, cartoons, and jokes for her eighty-two-year-old mother. Sharon has to keep finding it for her mother because her sisters and children keep taking it to read.

II

Humor and Gender
She Who Laughs, Lasts

I saved a marriage once. In my humor workshops, I invite participants to take something away that they can use in their lives. One recently married workshop attendee was upset when her hilarious pranks didn't seem to be funny to her husband. In fact, he was emphatically unappreciative of her efforts at humor. When I spoke about how we tend to give away our own humor instead of finding out what makes others laugh, suddenly the light bulb went on for her. She immediately understood why her prankster tricks weren't working with her husband. Not only did he not appreciate that kind of humor, she wasn't at all clear what actually made him laugh. The woman left the workshop intent on finding out. When we met again, she told me her humor relationship with her husband had improved immeasurably. She had discovered he was a punster. Now she enjoys finding puns that make him laugh.

Experiences like this keep me going in this business!

However, there also have been marriages that I could not save. For example, Cameron hired me as her humor coach because she wanted to lighten up. In truth, her husband, Keith, wanted her to lighten up. Committed as she was to being the best partner she could be, she came to me to learn how. For several weeks, she spent time getting to know his humor, creating opportunities to bring humor to their relationship as well as to the rest of her life. She had great success bringing humor to her relationship with her five-year-old son and to her work as a physician in a small town clinic.

During one of our conversations, she happened to mention her concerns about Keith's gambling. Having spent four years in the Professional Education Department at Hazelden, I understood how addictions could destroy relationships. I urged her to protect herself and her son and referred her to professionals who could help with that issue. As it turned out, my suspicions that Keith's gambling were at the root of the family's problems were confirmed. The family had been devastated financially by Keith's gambling and that he was unwilling to seek professional help. Cameron continues to lighten up and develop her humor *outside* that relationship.

Both of these examples illustrate an important lesson about humor and healthy relationships: humor is a tool, a means to an end, not the end itself. True intimacy requires a respectful, trusting relationship. Without the commitment to re-establish trust, Cameron's effort to lighten up within her relationship with Keith was doomed. Humor doesn't promote intimacy where there is distrust, disrespect or denial. Healthy humor is based on relational trust.

Why Doesn't He (or She) Get It?

While it is no surprise to most people that men and women are different from each other in a number of vitally important ways, the differences in how men and women view and express humor are not always well understood. Just as there are societal expectations about numerous other gender differences, there are also subtle variations in how men and women participate in humor.

One key difference: men have more permission to be funny than women have. Society expects men to perform. Being funny and clever is one type of performance. However, men also tend to laugh less, perhaps because male socialization teaches them that they must always be in control. According to Susan Horowitz in *Queens of Comedy*, "The most resistant audiences—for both male and female comics—are male, mainly because they equate laughter with losing control."

On the other hand, women have more permission (perhaps even pressure) to laugh. It makes them a better audience. Horowitz quotes comic Jerry Seinfeld, "They're more open. I've always felt an audience dominated by women is great for me because they don't have any withholds on getting silly and doing things for fun. A woman's sense of humor is much more free, open and loving—it doesn't have to make sense. If it's fun, great."

Indeed, women, even while they have been socialized to contain their own sense of humor, are led to believe they should laugh even if they don't think something is funny. They're told it's good to laugh at men's jokes, good to show a lighter side and support men's humor. And that may not be all bad. Dr. Madan Kataria, founder of the Laughter Club movement and author of *Laughter for No Reason*, states that even inauthentic or fake laughing delivers the same health benefits as the real deal. This may be one reason women live longer than men.

I'm tired of all this business about beauty being only skin deep. That's deep enough. What do you want—an adorable pancreas?
—Jean Kerr, writer

In *Honey Hush*, Daryl Cumber Dance describes how "proper ladies" are supposed to laugh. "Hold your hand over your mouth . . . hold it straight and a little to the side, like you're going to whisper something to someone next to you." Now women seem to be reclaiming their authenticity, consciously choosing when they will laugh and how. Perhaps that's one reason feminists are accused of not having a sense of humor.

A man asked the reference librarian where he could find the book, *The Male: The Superior Sex*. Immediately the librarian responded, "Oh, that would be over in fiction."

A couple of weeks ago a comedian complained to me it isn't fair that women can tell jokes about men and get away with it, but men can't tell jokes about women without being criticized. I wanted to tell him about the various theories on laughter as a weapon of the underdog—but it had too many words and no pictures. I told him that if all males would relinquish their power, eradicate rape from the face of the earth and give women twice as much money as men for the same job, then he could tell as jokes about women as he wanted. Until then, tough luck.
From Mary Hirsh, "Heard Any Good Jokes Lately?" *Minnesota Women's Press*

It's Time for Women to Stop Laughing Like Ladies!

Isn't it curious that while women laugh more than men, and are even socialized to laugh, they are often told, subtly and sometimes not so subtly, that they have no sense of humor?

Another way that men and women differ is in their opinions about what's funny. The British Association for the Advancement of Science conducted an experiment over the Internet. The results of this search for "the world's funniest joke" in which 350,000 people submitted and/or rated jokes were published in a book, *Laughlab*. According to the director, Dr. Richard Wiseman, an unintended result of the experiment was a more accurate understanding of the jokes preferred by each sex. Males favored jokes involving aggression, sexual innuendo and the put-down of women. Women preferred jokes involving word play. "These findings reflect fundamental differences in the way in which males and females use humour," Wiseman asserted. "Males use humour to appear superior to others, whilst women are more linguistically skilled and prefer word-puns."

Humor that uses aggression, sexual innuendo and the put-down of women—especially humor that uses all three—is not conducive to healthy relationships and, in fact, is harmful.

A difference in taste in jokes is a great strain on the affections.
—George Eliot, author

A study in the *Washington Post* says that women have better verbal skills than men. I just want to say to the authors of that study: "Duh."
—Conan O'Brien, late night talk show host
[Found on 15,000 Web sites]

Word play:
- **A Freudian slip is when you say one thing and mean your mother.**
- **When you dream in color, it's a pigment of your imagination.**
On 73 Web sites

In an article on humor in *Sexuality, Society, and Feminism*, Michael Mulkay examined the representation of women in men's sexual humor by analyzing dirty jokes collected by folklore researchers and comic routines in British pubs observed by ethnographers. He identified four basic themes in this male sexual humor:

1) The primacy of intercourse—all men want is sex.
2) The availability of women—all women are sexually available to all men even when they pretend not to be.
3) The objectification of women—women exist to meet men's needs, and are, or should be, passive.
4) The subordination of women's discourse—women must be silenced.

These themes articulate why this type of sexual humor is offensive and hurtful to women personally and also detrimental to healthy relationships between men and women. I want to be careful not to over-generalize from the two studies listed above, which reflect a fairly small segment of English-speaking males. However, the fact is that there is an over-abundance of jokes that reflect these themes. I will not provide examples here, and I assume you don't need to be convinced of the harm this kind of humor can do to relationships.

Nevertheless, we have to remember that some sexual humor can be healthy and appropriate. In the United States there seems to be a tendency to label humor either dirty or clean, with anything sexual belonging to the dirty category, thus perpetuating the unfortunate notion that sex is dirty. I am not opposed to humor with sexual innuendos, as long as it doesn't use the themes outlined above. Mulkay's identification of these themes can be useful in distinguishing between sexual humor that is harmful and that which is healthy.

There were three engineers discussing the design of the human body. The mechanical engineer insisted that it must have been a mechanical engineer who designed it since without the skeletal structure we would be like jellyfish. The electrical engineer claimed that an electrical engineer designed the body, given the importance of the brain and the nervous system. The civil engineer said, "No, no, no! It had to be a civil engineer. Who else

would put a waste-water treatment facility in the middle of a recreational area?

Cartoon from *Ma, can I be a feminist and still like men?* by Nicole Hollander   Used with permission

Beyond the differences in joke preferences between the sexes, Dr. Nancy Walker, a professor of women's studies and author of *A Very Serious Thing*, suggests that women don't particularly like jokes. In her study of women's literature, she found that women tend to be

Cartoon from *Ma, can I be a feminist and still like men?* by Nicole Hollander   Used with permission

storytellers rather than joke tellers. For women, humor functions as a means of communication rather than as a means of self-presentation, a sharing of experience rather than a demonstration of cleverness. Women more often prefer the spontaneous humor of everyday life, amusing stories, and anecdotes. They are more participatory. Walker identified the following common characteristics of women's written humor: it embodies a we/they attitude, reveals a collective consciousness, and makes clear that a group other than ourselves has made the rules by which we must live.

The late Erma Bombeck's writing exemplifies these characteristics. When women's lives were centered in the home, that was the primary source of humor for them. Erma Bombeck capitalized on it, and women loved her column. Men, whose lives were centered outside the home, didn't get Bombeck's humor. Males who have assumed more responsibility in the home now have a finer appreciation for her writing.

"The harder a woman works, the more things go wrong," Bombeck said about the perils of being a mother and a homemaker. According to Nancy Walker, Bombeck's humor created a sense of community for women, building women's confidence and identifying a social system that "makes women solely responsible for the functioning of the household and sets impossibly high standards for their performance."

Bombeck simply used humor to point out some of the same cultural incongruities and inequities that scholars were trying to expose. For example, in *Honey Hush: An Anthology of African American Women's Humor,* editor Daryl Cumber Dance presents dozens of examples of the characteristics Walker identifies: the we/they attitude, the collective consciousness, and the notion that a group other than African American women has made the rules by which they must live. She writes,

> Humor hasn't been for us so much the cute, the whimsical, and the delightfully funny. Humor for us has rather been a means of surviving as we struggled. We haven't been laughing so much because things tickle us. We laugh, as the old blues line declares, to keep from crying. We laugh to keep from dying. We laugh to keep from killing. We laugh to hide our pain, to walk gently around the wound too painful to actually touch. We laugh to shield our shame. We use our humor to speak the unspeak-

able, to mask the attack, to get a tricky subject on the table, to warn of lines not to be crossed, to strike out at enemies and the hateful acts of friends and family, to camouflage sensitivity, to tease, to compliment, to berate, to brag, to flirt, to speculate, to gossip, to educate, to correct the lies people tell on us, to bring about change.

How many people know what it's like to be the only person in a relationship?

—Linda Moakes, comedian

During my time in Studium (2002 to 2003), a residential scholars' program of the Sisters of Saint Benedict, I discovered I was living in a laugh laboratory. Where else could I find a better reflection of women's humor than in a women's monastery? My experience at monastery meals confirms the research; amusing stories of daily living are shared and everyone participates. Sometimes two or three people tell an anecdote together. You often hear words of encouragement: "Sister, tell the one about . . ." Here are two of my favorites:

When the sister known for her social justice work was speeding across Montana, a patrolman pulled her over. He asked, "Didn't you see me on the side of the road?" She said, "Yes." The officer asked why she didn't slow down. She innocently and honestly replied, "I thought it would be hypocritical."

Reprinted with permission

While assigning research topics, a sister theology professor announced, "Sexual intercourse hasn't been chosen; anyone interested in this topic, please see me in my office."

Reprinted with permission

Finally, although women are seldom included in standard anthologies of American humor, there are numerous anthologies of women's humor available. We have a richer written heritage than we may realize. Besides the books mentioned above, other favorites include: *They Used to Call Me Snow White But I Drifted*, *In Stitches*, *Pulling Our Strings*, *Women's Comic Visions*, *Women's Comic Fiction*, and *Redressing the Balance*.

How many have heard of best-selling writer, Marietta Holley? Holley wrote more than twenty books from 1873 to 1914. She was enormously popular and entertained as many people as Mark Twain. Through the wit and gentle satire of her main character, Samantha, wife of Josiah Allen, she challenged the status quo of social and political realities, especially concerning women's rights. For example, "Samantha cannot understand why men are trying so hard to protect women from the effort it takes to walk to the polling booth and slip a piece of paper in a box. She has noticed that these same protective instincts do not apply to churning butter, baking bread, and washing clothes, which she observes take considerably more effort."

www.northnet.org/stlawrenceaauw/holley

Appreciating Gender Differences

Men and woman look at things differently, experience humor differently. So, how can we appreciate gender differences in humor? Is there any hope?

Furthermore, how can humor be an opportunity to foster a greater understanding between the sexes? Are there differences that we do not want to appreciate, differences that, in fact, may be harmful to healthy relationships?

Humor can be a means to become closer to people, a tool for creating healthy relationships. As a form of communication, humor can be used constructively to build self-esteem or can be used to undermine it. It can serve as the road to reconciliation and an appreciation of the differences between men and women or it can provide ammunition for the battle of the sexes.

Humor can be a bonding experience, a sharing of experience, creating a sense of belonging, a sense of partnership. As a form of self-presentation and expression of cleverness, humor can be a valuable form of entertainment for the entertainer and the *entertainee*, a means for laughing, playing, and having fun together. It also can serve as an expression of love, a building block in the foundation for fun-loving, passionate, committed relationships.

In the words of the Russian novelist, Fyodor Dostoevsky: "If you wish to glimpse inside a human soul and get to know someone, don't bother analyzing their ways of being silent, of talking, of weeping, or seeing how much they are moved by noble ideas; you'll get better results if you just watch them laugh. If they laugh well, they're good people" (adapted to inclusive language).

Actor Joanne Woodward has another take on the importance of humor in relationships: "Sexiness wears thin after a while and beauty fades, but to be married to a man who makes you laugh every day, ah, now that's a real treat." Woodward has been married for forty-six years to my favorite blue-eyed actor, social activist and entrepreneur, Paul Newman.

"While attending a marriage seminar on communication, my husband and I listened to the instructor declare, 'It is essential that husbands and wives know the things that are important to each other.' He addressed the men. 'Can you describe your wife's goals, her dreams? Do you know her favorite song, her favorite flower?' My husband leaned over, touched my arm tenderly and whispered, 'Pillsbury All-Purpose, isn't it?'"

—Merrilyn Belgum

Ideas

Discuss ideas from this section with other men and women. Explore ways to encourage each other to be funny and to laugh uncontrollably.

After I shared my research on humor and gender, Patrick Henry, director of the Ecumenical Institute at St. John's University in Collegeville, Minnesota, mentioned his experience of being one of five men in an audience of 200 women at a conference on women and theology. He admitted not knowing when to laugh. He shared this with a woman at the conference who worked primarily with male clergy. She loved the experience. It was one of the few times she knew when to laugh.

Make a humor date. Have you ever done that on purpose? You might have fun making a list of activities for such an occasion. Here are some ideas:

- Go to a magic store and ask the clerk to demonstrate the products
- Invite a favorite comedian or funny friend to lunch
- Look for humor at an art museum
- Go for a drive or a walk in search of humor
- See how many funny stories you can collect from people you encounter
- Make people laugh
- Go shopping for things that make each other laugh
- Create your own humor scavenger hunt
- Volunteer together at a daycare center
- Invite funny friends to go on a double date
- List your favorite funny movies; then rent one

Once you have your list, put the items in a hat and draw one out. Or schedule a humor date and then create it.

A friend of mine has created a Valentine tradition. Throughout the year she collects Valentine gifts. At the party we take turns throwing a pair of dice. When you get a double, you choose a gift or you can steal one of the gifts already taken. The chocolate gifts are usually "stolen" most often. A time limit or a certain number of turns determines the end of the game.

Find out what makes others laugh. Make it a point to give them something that reflects their humor and not just yours. We often give away our humor instead of finding out what makes others laugh and giving them theirs. This is also a great way to discover new sources of humor. We've all heard of the Golden Rule: Do unto others as you want them to do unto you. Have you ever heard of the Platinum Rule? Do unto others as they want to be done unto. Give others what they want instead of what you want to give or what you think they should want.

Children's Version of Golden Rule: Do One to Others as they do One to You.

Play with Words

The *Washington Post* hosts a "Style Invitational," inviting readers to take any word from the dictionary and alter it by adding, subtracting or changing one letter, and then supply a new definition.

Here are some winning entries:

sarcasm becomes **sarchasm**
The gulf between the author of sarcastic wit and the recipient who doesn't get it

inoculate becomes **inoculatte**
The taking of coffee intravenously when you are running late

libido becomes **glibido**
All talk and no action

From a friend, Bruce Peck:

confide becomes **confido**
To tell a secret to your dog

decompose becomes **decomprose**
A rotten style of writing

disconsolate becomes **disconsolatte**
The sad feeling you get when you run out of coffee

echo becomes **echow**
A repeated request for food

Another word-play story:

My neighbor found out her dog could hardly hear, so she took it to the vet. He found the problem was hair in its ears and cleaned both ears, and the dog could hear fine. The vet told the lady if she wanted to keep this from reoccurring she should get some

"Nair" hair remover and rub it in its ears once a month. The lady went to the drug store to get some. At the register, the druggist tells her, "If you're going to use Nair under your arms don't use deodorant for a few days." The lady says, "I'm not using it under my arms." The druggist says, "If you're using it on your legs, don't shave for a couple of days." The lady says, "I'm not using it on my legs either, and if you must know I'm using it on my schnauzer." The druggist looked at her in amusement and cautioned, "Stay off your bicycle for a week."   Found on over 300 Web sites

Write a fun personal ad. If you are already with a partner, write one for each other. Write what you think your partner wants in a mate. Compare ads.

Senior Personal Want Ads:

WINNING SMILE: Active grandmother with original teeth seeking a dedicated flosser to share rare steaks, corn on the cob, and caramel candy.

MINT CONDITION: Male, 1922, high mileage, good condition, some hair, many new parts including hip, knee, cornea, valves. Isn't in running condition, but walks well.

On over 300 Web sites

III

Laugh and Love Your Family

When he was younger, my son, Jesse, and I always kept a pair of Groucho glasses in the car—you know, the kind with the giant nose and bushy, black eyebrows and mustache. My son entertained himself and other people who pulled up alongside us on the freeway. His responses delighted me. One day he said, "Business people are too serious!" I said in mock defensiveness, "Well, I'm a business person!" He replied, "But, Mom, you're a business person who does fun for a living."

Jesse, age three   Photo by Jeremy deFiebre

In my humor work, I urge grown-ups to use funny glasses, too. When I find myself behind a bus or a station wagon with young people waving their hands or making faces, I don a pair of goofy glasses and watch their reaction. Shaking up young people's expectations of who we are as adults is a hoot! In addition, it makes my long drives seem shorter.

How many times do children laugh each day? I have seen a variety of answers to that question: 146, 200, 300, and 400. My hunch is that the number goes down as our age goes up. The number quoted most often for how many times adults laugh is a dozen times a day. I have an accounting friend, Jill, who keeps track. She is above average. For example, while previewing this book, she reported laughing out loud twenty-nine times.

According to Dolores Curran in *Traits of a Healthy Family*, a sense of humor and play is one of the traits of a healthy family, whatever its arrangement. Trusting in ourselves as parents is crucial to be effective in adding humor and play to family life. We all want to be the best parents we can be. When we are preoccupied with getting it right or looking good, we lose our sense of humor and miss out on many opportunities to give and receive humor with our children. One of the greatest rewards of my work comes when parents lighten up with their children.

When my son was eight or nine years old, he often invited me to play Nintendo. I declined. I was an anti-Nintendo mom, and I didn't think that form of play was valuable. I thought he should be playing with people rather than machines. One day I realized he was eagerly trying to contribute to the enjoyment of my life, and I was not being open to his contribution. I learned how to play and enjoy Dr. Mario, a Nintendo game. Pretty soon, he was telling me I was spending too much time in front of the television, playing Nintendo.

Learning to downhill ski was also a joy for me. When I drove Jesse to the slopes to ski, he would urge me to ski with him. I was content to watch from the chalet. It was such fun as he taught me how to get on and off the ski lift. I specifically recall the conversation in the car on the way to my first ski lesson. He shared with me his frustration with grown-ups who budge in front of children waiting in the checkout line at the store. I explained that sometimes adults treat children the way they were treated. He turned to me and said, "Well, you must have been treated pretty good then." I passed that compliment on to my mother.

One of the best investments we can make in the future is to do whatever it takes to increase our confidence as parents. One critical ingredient for lightening up as parents is the recognition that our parents/caretakers did the best they could with the resources they had.

In a powerful transformational education program through Landmark Education, I realized at the age of forty-two, that I still wanted my mother to be who I wanted her to be. I hadn't realized that I was making her wrong for not teaching me how to relax. She did teach me how to work hard, for which I am grateful. I would not be where I am today without that ability. Now I have the privilege of giving my eighty-five-year-old mother permission to relax.

In letting go of the past, specifically the expectations for my mother, I took responsibility for my life and lightened up in my parenting—not expecting myself or my son to be perfect. I will never forget one mother saying, "There are plenty of therapists out there." She was admitting publicly that she was not going to be the perfect parent. Our children will have their own stuff with which to deal.

The harder we try to be perfect and expect them to be perfect, the less we will enjoy our children. In fact, the notions we have—the ways we think we should be perfect—can be a great source of humor. Learn to laugh at those notions, e.g., we should always have clean clothes on our children; we should be polite and have children so trained to behave in public that they don't grab food off another's plate, and we should be in control and not give in to tantrums.

We often get frustrated when our young children ask too many questions. We seldom stop to consider that sometimes we do the same thing to them. A mother offered this experience of asking too many questions:

My three-year-old son had a lot of problems with potty training and I was on him constantly. One day we stopped at Taco Bell for a quick lunch in between errands. It was very busy, with a full dining room. While enjoying my taco, I smelled something funny, so I checked my seven-month-old daughter, and she was clean. Then I realized that Matt had not asked to go potty in a while, so I asked him, and he said, "No." I thought, "Oh Lord,

that child has had an accident and I don't have any extra clothes with me." Then I said, "Matt, are you sure you didn't have an accident?" "No," he replied irritably. I just knew that he must have because the smell was getting worse. Soooo . . . I asked one more time, "Matt, did you have an accident?" This time he jumped up, yanked down his pants, bent over and spread his cheeks and yelled, "SEE, MOM, IT'S JUST FARTS!!"

While 100 people nearly choked to death on their tacos, he calmly pulled up his pants and sat down to eat his food as if nothing happened. I was mortified . . . until some kind elderly people made me feel a lot better when they came over and thanked me for the best laugh they had ever had!

On over 20,000 Web sites

Right after my son became an adult, I finally figured out adolescent humor. That's the way it is with parenting; just when we begin to understand what is going on with our children, they catapult to the next stage. In my experience, many adolescents love to watch and recount the stupid things adults say and do. Seek to keep a light heart as teenagers laughingly point out your eccentricities, flaws, and frailties. Remember that we are very funny to them, as our parents were also very funny to us. In fact, my best advice to parents of teens: hold tight to your sense of humor. You will need it.

In *776 Stupidest Things Ever Said*, **Ross and Kathryn Petras include:**

"A verbal contract isn't worth the paper it is written on."

—Samuel Goldwyn, movie mogul

"The streets are safe in Philadelphia; it is only the people who make them unsafe."
—Frank Rizzo, mayor

"During a state of national emergency resulting from enemy attack, the essential functions of the Service will be as follows: (1) assessing, collecting and recording taxes . . ."

Internal Revenue Service, 1976

Laughlab, **a book based on the experiment on the Internet, reports the following as the top joke by people aged eleven to** fifteen: A new teacher was trying to make use of her psychology courses. She started her class by saying: "Everyone who thinks they're stupid, stand up!" After a few seconds, Little Johnny stood up. The teacher said: "Do you think you're stupid, Little Johnny?" Little Johnny replied: "No ma'am, but I hate to see you standing there all by yourself."

An example of my adolescent humor is the nude statue joke, which I have been telling since tenth grade. Here is how I remember it: There were these two nude statues in the park, one male, one female. Suddenly, through some miracle, the statues came to life. The female nude said to the male nude, "Wow! I've been waiting for this chance for so long." The male nude said to the female nude, "Wow! I've been waiting for this chance for so long, too." They linked hands and ran through the park pooping on all the birds.

It seems we don't have to remind grandparents to enjoy children. Grandparents bring a greater freedom and acceptance of themselves and the children. Although there are big differences between parenting and grandparenting, we don't need to wait until we are grandparents to enjoy children.

(ASIDE - When I typed the word "grandparenting," spell check gave me a choice between hyphenating it "grand·parent·ing" or "grandpa· rent·ing." Even spell check likes wordplay.)

I encourage people to allow parents and grandparents to tell funny stories about their children and grandchildren even if "you had to be there." I especially like to give single parents the opportunity to tell stories of their children. One of the greatest losses in single parenting is not having someone with whom to share the funny experiences.

Some people think of themselves as humorless—especially if they didn't grow up in a funny family. It is never too late to have a happy childhood. Every family's sense of fun is different. Some tell stories around the supper table while others play cooperative games or board games, engage in scavenger hunts or perform skits at family reunions. Think about how

Single Slices / Peter Kohlsaat

I have to spend quality time with my parents or they'll become dysfunctional.

Reprinted with permission

you might build opportunities for humor and play in your family gatherings.

I mailed the cartoon (at right) to my twenty-three-year-old son with an invitation to eat at his favorite restaurant. This is one way I remind him that I love him. The florist says, "Say it with flowers." The humorist says, "Say it with humor." The point is, "Say it!"

Tell your family and friends that you love them in whatever way works.

Two slogans from Gay Pride T-shirts:
My Mommies Love Me
Love Makes a Family

When Jesse was born, instead of the traditional baby book, we received a blank book to record the funny things he said and did. The following are two entries:

When Jesse, age six, visited his friend Dylan, the lunch conversation somehow made its way to the subject of head-cheese, which is quite literally made from the meat in a pig's head, including the brains. Someone, of course, commented about food for thought. Jesse piped up, "Seems to me it's food *that* thought." He didn't realize it was funny until the grown-ups started laughing.

About a year later, Jesse and I were sitting outside with lots of grasshoppers hopping around us. I said to him, "I wonder what that brown juice is that grasshoppers spit?" Jesse quipped, "Oh, I could look that up in my *insectlopedia*." This time he knew he was making a joke. And, of course, he had an appreciative audience.

Children of all ages love to laugh and hear others laugh and, happily for them, they don't feel inhibited by social etiquette. I miss that old Art Linkletter show, *Kids Say the Darndest Things.* Bill Cosby's program by the same name was also good.

Children's humor is perhaps the most popular and safest to share in public and via e-mail. The following witty wisdom is kids teaching us about love.

When asked what people do on dates, one little guy replied, "On the first day they just tell each other lies that get them interested enough to go on a second date."

When asked what is the proper age to get married, Judy, age eight, says, "Eighty-four, because at that age, you don't have to work anymore, and you can spend all your time loving each other in your bedroom." Five-year-old Tom took a stance opposite of Judy with his answer, "Once I'm done with kindergarten, I'm going to find me a wife."

When he was asked about the role of good looks in love, Gary, age seven, proclaimed, "It isn't always just how you look. Look at me. I'm handsome like anything and I haven't got anybody to marry me yet." On over 1,900 Web sites

Playful pet   Photo by Barbara La Valleur

Ideas

Look for the humor in everyday life. Be surprised by what shows up. I thought it was funny when someone pointed out that in the 1990 tax booklet (Form 1040), "embezzled and other illegal income" was listed under "Income You Must Report." (The IRS has since taken it out of the 1040 booklet.)

Church signs:
- CHURCH PARKING—FOR MEMBERS ONLY! Trespassers will be baptized.
- Free Trip to Heaven. Details Inside!
- How will you spend eternity—Smoking or Non-smoking?
- Come, work for the Lord. The work is hard, the hours are long and the pay is low. But the retirement benefits are out of this world.

On 61 Web sites

Another source of humor is reading the labels on products. Enjoy these classics:

On a hair dryer: Do not use while sleeping.
On a bag of chips: You could be a winner. No purchase necessary. Details inside.
Directions on a bar of soap: Use like regular soap.
On the packaging for an iron: Do not iron clothes on body.

Keep colorful or cartoon **Band-Aids** around. When someone is in pain, the cartoons are a good distraction. The Band-Aids are also useful reminders to be kind to yourself, instead of placing a string around your finger.

Spend time with your children and your grandparents, your own or someone else's, volunteer at a childcare center or become a Big Brother or Sister. Visit a nursing home. Our elders can be great sources for giving and receiving humor.

Pet humor: many people enjoy the antics of their pets and share them with others. With permission take your pets when you visit a nursing home or childcare center.

Goat with an attitude   Photo by Barbara La Valleur

Play with exaggeration—another idea for developing your sense of humor. Some storytellers use exaggeration; children particularly love it. Invite them to tell exaggerated stories with you. The late actress Lucille Ball was an expert on exaggeration. If you haven't seen the *I Love Lucy* shows in the candy factory, stomping the grapes or advertising Vitameenavegamins, put them on your "to-see-immediately" list. Then follow her example.

In *The Healing Power of Humor*, Allen Klein devotes a whole chapter to exaggeration, as a "simple technique for making painful moments laughable." When upset, write an overstated, exaggerated letter. Klein suggests exaggerating your feelings until they become so absurd you begin to laugh. "If you are already having a bad day, then *really* have one. Complain endlessly about how rotten your day is, how uncooperative everyone is, how nasty your boss is (not to mention dumb, ugly and stingy). Pretend you are in the Oh-What-an-Awful-Day Olympics and that you desperately want to win a gold medal. Jump up and down, throw a temper tantrum, crawl on the floor and cry like a baby." He recommends discretion on where you practice this exercise.

Another idea from Klein: carry a get-out-of-jail-free card next to your driver's license. When stopped by the police, give them your get-out-of-jail-free card. Don't blame me if you choose to do this and it backfires.

Give the gift of humor. Give a blank book as a baby gift for parents to record their child's antics.

A white elephant gift exchange is fun. It could be for New Year's, Valentine's Day or whatever you are celebrating. It has become a tradition in our family to have a white elephant exchange instead of exchanging expensive Christmas gifts. This is how it works. Everyone brings a wrapped gift which can be any old or new thing found around the house, garage, yard, wherever—useful or not, funny or not. Some of us bring extra ones. It is fun to collect them throughout the year. We number pieces of paper (for the number of persons) and each person draws from a hat until all numbers are distributed. The person with number "1" chooses and unwraps a gift. The person with number "2"

Laugh and Love Your Family

can steal that gift or open another one. In numeric order, the rest of the people can take any opened gift or choose a new one until they have all been opened. If your gift is stolen, you get to open a new one. It is all done in good fun. Be careful about including youngsters who are unwilling to give up their gift. We include the younger family members by having extra white elephant presents just for them; no stealing allowed.

Some people get very creative with this type of gift-giving, such as wrapping up a "tax shelter"—a little building with a couple of tacks inside. Another punster brought the perfect gift for the parent of a teenager: a "phoneless" cord. Each year I have fun seeking out a white elephant—stuffed or ceramic.

Prankster in the family: My friend, Sister Ione Jesh, told about her brother who graciously offered to put the names in a hat for the drawing for the Christmas gift exchange. They had a good laugh when they realized they had all drawn his name.

The Eleventh Commandment: Humor thy father and mother.

Nature's umbrellas, naturally amusing   Photo by Barbara La Valleur

49

IV

Workplace Humor
Take This Job and Love It

The brain is a wonderful organ. It starts the moment you get up in the morning and does not stop until you get to work.

—Robert Frost, author

While running for president, John F. Kennedy was shaking hands at a factory gate in West Virginia. One grizzled worker asked him, "Is it true, young fellow, that you have a rich daddy and didn't have to work for a living if you didn't choose to?" Kennedy replied, "It's true. I have a rich daddy, and didn't have to work for a living." The worker shook his head and said, "Believe me, young fellow, you didn't miss a damn thing."

Adapted from Esther Blumenfeld and Lynn Alperne, *Humor at Work: The Guaranteed, Bottom-Line, Low-Cost, High Efficiency Guide to Success through Humor*

Plato asked, "What, then, is the right way of living?" His response was that life must be lived as play, "playing the noblest of games." What is the right way of working? Response: To experience work as play is the best. "The irony of all play is that it can be turned into work," writes Conrad Hyers in his book, *The Spirituality of Comedy*. Likewise, the irony of work is that it can also be a form of play. Earlier I told the story of my son calling me a business person who does fun for a living. I love the fact that he recognized it and that, even as a ten-ager (not a typo), he knew that what was fun for a living for me was not fun for him. At age twenty-three, he is happy as a plumber's apprentice.

Workplace Humor

Work and play are words used to describe the same thing under differing circumstances.
—Mark Twain, humorist

What would you do if you had a rich daddy or mommy and didn't have to work for a living? How would you define "fun for a living"? If you want more humor in your work life, one place to begin is the level of happiness and satisfaction in your work. Humor is a diagnostic tool that indicates whether you are in the right work and in the right workplace.

If you asked me what I came to do in this world, I, an artist, will answer you: I am here to live out loud.
—Emile Zola, novelist

Irish Blessing: Work like you don't need money, love like you've never been hurt and dance like no one's watching.

In my first career, two co-workers confronted me about my lack of happiness. At first I did not trust them. I thought they were just trying to get rid of me. When I read my journal for the previous few weeks, I realized that what they said was true. I was unhappy at work and they were experiencing it as well. I had lost my sense of humor and my effectiveness in working with others. My unhappiness and my distrust of my co-workers was a clear indication that it was time for me to find other work.

At another point in my work career, my unhappiness and dissatisfaction was due to the high level of turmoil at home and at work. My child was young, my marriage was in trouble, and there was a fair amount of stress at work. My attempt to be Supermom, Superspouse, and Superworker wasn't working. My sense of humor was at a low point. The stress in my life was at a high point. I gave up my job in order to salvage my marriage and my humor. When it became clear that my marriage was not going to work out, I chose work that supported my well-being and my relationship with my son, even though it involved a major cut in pay.

After five years I was down-sized, laid off, given the pink slip. By then I was in a better position to take a risk, so I started my own business. Now my level of happiness, like my sense of humor, is high on most days. Because of the level of satisfaction I experience with my work, I am able to continue to take risks, like taking time to write this book.

Clearly the key to having humor at work is ensuring a minimum level of satisfaction with that work, or at the very least, a minimum level of overall happiness. Recently I heard about both a small-town undertaker and an academic dean who took up clowning on the side. If you increase your happiness in other areas of life, it will likely have a positive effect on your work.

It is important to choose one's attitude on a daily basis. Even though I do fun for a living, there are days when my work is a struggle. On those days, I often phone a friend to get in touch with the possibility of play in my work. The distinction between work and play has more to do with our attitudes, feelings and perceptions about work than with the actual work we are doing. The classic example is Tom Sawyer's response when given the chore of painting the fence. He successfully creates for his friends such a glorious picture of how much fun it is to paint a fence that they end up paying him for the opportunity to do the work. Admittedly, payment is made in frogs and other pocket change, but it's payment, nonetheless.

As I mentioned, earlier in my career, I was a professional education specialist at Hazelden. My responsibilities included designing and facilitating workshops for health care professionals. When we took our workshops on the road, I was responsible for the travel details including lodging arrangements and classroom set up. Once I traveled to Denver with the former president of Hazelden to deliver an Employee Assistance workshop. When we checked into the hotel, the clerk informed us that we were both registered in the same room. Without skipping a beat, Jerry turned to me and said, "Nice try, Linda," making an embarrassing situation even more embarrassing.

BLAMESTORMING: sitting around in a group, discussing why a deadline was missed or a project failed, and who was responsible.

On 448 Web sites

Work Culture

Just as humor will not work when there is distrust and denial within a relationship, trust and respect are crucial to healthy humor in a workplace. If upper management fails to walk the talk, employees will grumble, even about humor in the workplace. The FISH video about the Pike Place Fish market in Seattle is a very popular training video produced by Charthouse Learning. The four themes of this customer service video are 1) play, 2) choose your attitude, 3) make their day, and 4) be there.

I occasionally hear complaints that management is merely giving lip service to the "fish philosophy." If employees do not feel respected, it's obvious that managers are not practicing what is preached in the video. The employees of Pike Place Fish are all playing at work. It is obvious that they are having fun, that they enjoy their work, and there is mutual respect between employees and the owners of the market. Their mission is more than selling fish; they practice internal and external customer service. I believe we treat our customers the way we are treated, which is another indicator of a healthy workplace.

Ben and Jerry's, the ice cream people, is another company that demonstrates appreciation for the benefits of humor and their regard for the well-being of employees. The company has a Joy Committee that is assigned a budget line. Their three mission statements include a commitment to a quality product and respect for the environment, a commitment to a certain level of profitability and an intention to improve the quality of life locally, nationally and internationally. Their slogan is "One Sweet Whirled" (say this aloud to get the pun). It's a commitment to cause a different kind of global warming—with ice cream! [www.benjerry.com]

Southwest Airlines is another company known for fun and play in the workplace. There are several Web sites with airline humor, particularly humor used to reduce the stress during take-off and landing.

After a bone-jarring landing, a Southwest Airlines attendant said over the intercom: "That was quite a bump, and I know what ya'll are thinking. I'm here to tell you it wasn't the airline's fault, it wasn't the pilot's fault, and it wasn't the flight attendants' fault. It was the asphalt."

53

"As we prepare for take-off, please make sure your tray tables and seat backs are fully upright and in their most uncomfortable position."

"Smoking in the lavatories is prohibited. Any person caught smoking in the lavatories will be asked to leave the plane immediately."

"Last one off the plane must clean it."

And from the pilot during his welcome message: "We are pleased to have some of the best flight attendants in the industry. Unfortunately none of them are on this flight!"

On over 100,000 Web sites

If we assume that humor is an important part of the work environment, can we also use humor as a useful diagnostic tool for evaluating workplace health? Of course! Often we are critical of the ways individuals use humor at work. It certainly is one kind of behavior in which we may have significant differences. In fact, if you are being interviewed for a position, you might consider asking questions about how the company views and fosters humor. This can provide valuable indicators of the health of the organization and whether it's the right place for you. Here are a few questions to consider.

1. Is there a clear mission for the company or organization? Is it clearly projected, and are people aligned behind that mission?
2. What are the values of the company? Are the values consistent with fostering healthy humor and play?
3. Is its humor lighthearted or depressing? Is it sarcastic and cynical or friendly and playful?
4. Is the humor open or secretive—behind people's backs?

Fortunately, many companies are overthrowing the myth that workers can't have fun and still be productive. There is an ever-growing body of research indicating that a sense of humor is one important quality of a healthy workplace. Employees who have fun at work are more creative and productive; they organize data better, solve problems more quickly and make stronger decisions. According to Terry Braverman in "Enhance Your Sense of Self-Mirth," in *Training and Development*, in a survey of 329 executives, ninety-seven percent agreed that humor is a valuable asset in business; sixty percent considered it to be a decisive indicator of the success of a person in business. In another survey, eighty-four percent of human resource directors indicated that employees with a sense of humor perform better at work.

Statistics like these sometimes are used to convince employers of the need for humor in the workplace.

Which employer would you choose?

A. *"You have a right to enjoy life but only on your own time,"* an aphorism by Ashleigh Brilliant (www.AshleighBrilliant.com).

B. The one who recognizes that *"Employers ought to be begging to help people find the most enjoyable, fulfilling, and creative ways to do their work,"* from C.W. Metcalf, consultant and author.

Ninety-seven point three percent of all statistics are made up, including this one.

Inappropriate Seriousness

When I present programs on humor in the workplace, a common concern often emerges. People want me to answer the question: What is the difference between appropriate and inappropriate humor? Without minimizing that, I suggest there is a consideration of equal concern: What is appropriate and inappropriate seriousness? Inappropriate seriousness may be as prevalent as inappropriate humor.

Where does this concern come from? When white males were the major stockholders of companies, white male humor was the acceptable norm. As the demographics of the workplace continue to change—as there is more diversity in leadership positions in companies—the "humor norm" is likewise changing. What was deemed acceptable humor at one time is no longer acceptable, and a keener awareness of diversity in humor is necessary.

Allen Klein developed what he calls the "AT&T check" for determining the appropriateness of humor. Klein asserts that humor must be appropriate, tasteful and timely. These criteria are often different for each workplace. Before giving a presentation on humor, I find someone within the organization to help me understand what is acceptable within his or her environment. This is crucial. The boundaries of appropriateness are tighter within the actual work setting than they seem to be when I'm presenting to a similar audience outside the work setting, such as a conference or professional association meeting.

Humor is a tool not only for diagnosing the health of a corporate culture, but also in creating a healthy work environment. There are ways to contribute to the health of a workplace, creating a greater sense of team and enhancing individual contributions:

- Refrain from sarcasm (the root word means to "tear flesh") at work, especially about individuals or the company.
- Always seek to distinguish whether you are laughing at or laughing with someone. This is profoundly important.
- Suggest that your company host a humor workshop to establish your own criteria for a healthy humor culture. When everyone at a work site has the opportunity to participate in establishing the criteria, they are more likely to respect humor guidelines.

Appreciating Differences with Humor

While leading team-building activities within a company, I let them know that teamwork is a relatively new term within work cultures. If you look at how long people have been on the planet, the word "teamwork" was introduced only in the last few decades. I urge people to be patient with themselves and each other. We are still finding our way. The fact that teamwork is a relatively new concept does not mean that people have not had to work together effectively in the past. The industrial model was not based on teamwork. My experience of teamwork is that team members want to do their part. We might complain about the speed of a co-worker or the amount of their output, but I believe that most workers want to do a good job.

We can take teamwork to the next level by imagining a workplace where everyone is out to make everyone a winner. Humor is a critical element in creating a win-win workplace.

One way to begin creating a winning work culture is to appreciate not only the various contributions of co-workers but also the differences in work styles. By taking a lighter approach to our differences, we are more able to understand them. Behaviors that irritate us can be recognized for their contribution, and variety in preferences can become a way to foster teamwork. That is why I advocate the use of learning instruments such as the MBTI (Myers Briggs Type Instrument), or the DiSC (Direct, interactive, Steady, Cautious) Personal Profile. (I am an Inscape Publisher distributor of the DiSC profile.) These tools are immeasurably useful in teaching people how to understand and appreciate differences in behavior. When we are working with people who operate differently than we do, we often lose our sense of humor. We think others should behave the same way we do, perform tasks the same way we do and care about the same things we do. The minute we leave humor behind, we become defensive, and misunderstandings escalate.

The first time I completed the DiSC Personal Profile, I was shocked to discover that not everyone was as preoccupied with being liked as I am. Some people are largely concerned with producing results. Others want quality. Some seek stability in their work environment. Understanding these differences creates an environment for respectful workplace humor.

Differences in behavioral styles can be a great source for laughter at work. Throughout these education programs, the task-oriented people gain an increasing appreciation for the relationship-oriented people and vice versa. The potential sources of irritation become potential sources of humor.

Insights from such a learning instrument helped the administrator of a health clinic discover that she was driving her managers crazy with her tendency to think aloud with them. She asked them whether there were any of her behaviors they did not understand. They articulated their frustration with her ambiguous self-talk. In fact, they confessed to leaving her office often with no idea what she expected from them. They were all able to laugh together as the administrator acknowledged the confusion and stress her behavior caused. She requested that her managers ask for clarification of her expectations when they felt frustrated.

In one of my workshops, the manager of a human resources team in a veterans' hospital explained that she learned how to greet her team members in the morning. She fostered a positive start to the day by not interrupting the task-oriented folks and personally greeting the relationship-oriented people. It was an adjustment that helped her to start each day on the right foot.

How we relate to rules is another behavioral difference that is often a source of workplace stress. Some people view rules as the absolute law, while others use rules as only general guidelines; still others simply resent rules altogether. Rule interpretation even manifests itself during card and board games.

"Eveything is funny, as long as it is happening to someone else."
—Will Rogers, humorist

A key to human understanding is viewing others' behaviors with an open mind and seeking to see the world through someone else's eyes. While I have already professed the usefulness of behavioral learning profiles, I also believe you can learn how to lighten up about behavioral differences at home or in the workplace on your own. All you need is the courage to actively communicate, asking those around you what they need from you. Out of these types of workplace conversations grow insight, mutuality, and respect.

Interrupting Gossip

Gossip Free Zone

Finally, gossip is an insidious poison in the workplace. I have a poster that superimposes the word "gossip" with the universal symbol for NO, a circle and slash, and the saying "Gossip Free Zone."

Encourage gossipers to take their concerns to a manager or someone who can do something about the situation or individual.

When I hear that someone has been gossiping about my business, I naturally want to tell them to mind their own business. It might be funnier if I said, "Great! Mind my business. You do it. I am willing to retire." It might diffuse frustration by coming up with hilarious responses to a gossip's probes even if you never use them.

> *"Live in such a way that you would not be ashamed to sell your parrot to the town gossip."*
>
> —Will Rogers, humorist

Ideas

Read *Humor at Work: the Guaranteed, Bottom-Line, Low-Cost, High-Efficiency Guide to Success through Humor* by Esther Blumenfeld and Lynn Alperne. This book lives up to its title. Blumenfeld and Alperne write about using humor to improve speeches and negotiations, to develop management and leadership abilities. Besides chapters on specific professions, they include an extensive resource list of conferences, organizations, and publications.

Meetings: Before starting my own business, I worked at a camp and conference center in the forest. Once we devoted a whole staff meeting to humor. I invited everyone on the staff of forty to bring something that reflected their own sense of humor. People told stories and jokes. They sang songs. One person drew a cartoon on a flipchart. The food service did "food art," using vegetables to create caricatures of individual staff people. Individuals were free to choose to pass. At this point Don Blackhawk, a Winnebago elder, told a story about the silly things people have said to indigenous people. It was the BEST staff meeting ever, especially for building community.

Bob Lichen, a real fungi

Food art drawing by Corinne Dwyer.

As a result, we included humor on the agenda of our all-staff meetings. Even five minutes made a difference. I found a Candid Camera video at the library and chose a five-minute clip of four-year-old children trying to remember phone messages for grown-ups. It was particularly fitting for us since we took turns answering the phone during meal times. We could see ourselves and each other in those little children.

I encourage people to team up when offering humor at meetings. Then, if you don't get the response you want, at least you aren't alone. Check out this great resource for enlivening meetings: *Energize Your Meetings* by Sheila Feigelson.

Give the gift of humor at work. Humorous calendars make great gifts. Recycle the calendar cartoons; include them in your correspondence or when you pay your bills. Give gift certificates for movies, a mystery tour, a joke a week, humor breaks or favorite places to play: water slides, ski slopes, bowling, golfing, or curling. (Make sure they take you along.)

Other ideas and examples of humor at work:
- Schedule humor breaks. Call someone up and tell a funny short story or ask for one. One friend who works for a rural medical center invites co-workers into the hallway for a two-minute laughter break.
- Hold a story hour once a month; let people tell happy or humorous stories that are important to them.
- Humorous e-mails—treat with caution—be selective and do this sparingly. Print and send them to people who don't have e-mail. I send them to my mom, who thoroughly enjoys getting humor in the mail.
- Potluck lunches—invite each person to bring food that reflects their sense of humor: i.e., corn nuts, hot dogs, or Cheerios. You might want to provide a few staples. When I did this with one work group, they supplied a hoagie sandwich as the staple.
- Have a real brown bag lunch where people go out on the lawn or nearby park and enjoy getting away from the phones and computers.
- Have a bagel-tasting contest with every conceivable idea of bagels and cream cheese.
- Conduct a field trip to another part of your organization. Combine it with a potluck.

- Put on a fun, educational skit at your next business meeting or conference. A friend organized an FBU, Funny Business Unit, in a computer firm. He and his friends acted out skits at company events and created a fun video for recruiting employees.
- Create a toy basket. Have stress reliever toys on the table during serious discussions and meetings.
- Sponsor an Art Week when employees can bring and display their own art. Or a Kids' Art Day when people bring in their kids' and grandkids' art. Be sure to display kid art on refrigerators!
- An artist friend, Sister Dennis Frandrup, submitted an annual report that included the doodles she had made on the notes of departmental meetings through-out the year. The graphics made it more interesting and playful. Her doodles are suitable for framing.

Sister Dennis Frandrup, doodler

- Instead of the ubiquitous baby picture contest, in which each person brings a baby picture and everyone guesses who is who, why not use pictures of pets and ask everyone to guess whose pet is whose. If you don't have a pet, cut out a picture of a pet you would have if you had a pet or bring a photo of your favorite houseplant. (Give people the freedom to pass.)
- Buy funny post-its or create your own with a Post-It Glue Stick.
- Put up funny posters in your office or cubicle.
- Invite a comedian or humor educator to your next conference or company celebration. (I'm available, and I'm good, ha!)
- When people retire or move on from your workplace, send them off with a funny "home" video of the workplace.
- Create a humorous bulletin board. Take turns changing it every two or three weeks.
- Celebrate holidays and create your own theme days such as Old Movies, Trivia, Chocolate, Hawaiian Luau. Brainstorm a list of ideas specific to your business. Sponsor a Happy Mirthday party in the middle of the most stressful season. (Mirth means merriment.)

- One family-oriented hotel offers clown training to employees who in turn entertain customers and the public.

Take up clowning with your children.   Photo by Sharon Henneman

- Play with props in the workplace: I use hand clappers, three hard plastic hands that clap together. It is great fun to "give people a hand" or "pat on the back" for a job well done, whether it is good customer service or recognition of a co-worker.

    One day when I was visiting my mother, she hosted a meeting of the Helping Hand Club at her home. I had a bag of hand clappers in my car, and as the members left the meeting, I gave each one a hand clapper. The club members laughed and loved it. Months later they are still talking about it.

V

Laugh and the Whole World Laughs with You

**During one of the Cold War Summit meetings, the partici-
pants were at a stalemate. Someone suggested that each person
tell a funny story. One of Russians posed this riddle: "What is the
difference between capitalism and communism?" The answer: "In
capitalism, man exploits man. In communism, it's the other way
around." I like to think that this is a true story, and that it made
a difference in ending the Cold War.** On sixty Web sites

Personal History

While growing up in rural Minnesota, my first experience of
challenging "the system" was confronting discrimination against farm
kids. My social studies teacher made snide remarks about farm kids
not being smart. My sense was that farm kids had more chores to do,
less time for homework and perhaps less patience with seemingly
irrelevant homework. I chose to stay in his class to prove him wrong,
since I excelled in social studies. I doubt I made any difference in his
attitude, but I felt better.

In college, I participated in student government, attended a
Student Power Conference (1968) and advocated for relevancy in
course content and student-centered learning. After college, my

63

activism continued in my work at the Education Exploration Center promoting parent and student participation in shaping the content and process of education at all levels.

Until college, I never saw a person of color. Since it was a big step for me to leave home, I chose a small, Catholic, women's college. My college "Big Sister" was from Africa and the first person of color I met. I'm embarrassed to admit that I don't even remember her name. Later, I became friends with Elda, a classmate from Nicaragua, and traveled to her home one summer. It was my first experience of the disparity between rich and poor.

While I was working at the Education Exploration Center, teacher and author Miriam Wasserman invited me to move to San Francisco to work with her on a book about education for social change—Midwest farmers' daughter meets New York Jewish grand-mother. It was a challenge for us to appreciate our cultural differences. However, together we produced *Teaching Human Dignity* (THD), an anthology written by teachers from around the country on education for social change (over 10,000 copies sold).

Although my work on THD expanded my knowledge of various minority groups, working at Wilder Forest was my first real experience of getting to know people of color, gays and lesbians, and people with disabilities as people—appreciating the similarities and differences in our lives.

Now I have the privilege and joy of working with Vicki Gee-Treft, who is Chinese and German, and Eustolio Benavides, a "Texan Mexican." We laugh a lot and love working together delivering culturally appropriate customized training. We don't pretend to have the answers. We do have a commitment to building a world that works for everyone and to have fun in the process. If the world is not working for one of us, it is not working for any of us.

Humor and Culture

Humor is a tool for transformation, a tool for thriving—not just surviving—as we create a world that works for everyone. By transforming our current paradigms, humor becomes a tool for building bridges across cultures and educating each other about peace and

Eustolio, me, and Vicki   Photo by Barbara La Valleur

justice issues. A paradigm is the way people perceive the world, e.g., at one time earth was viewed as flat. Many of us are in the process of shifting paradigms about the role of humor and play in working for peace and justice and creating a world that celebrates diversity of all kinds while building community among all people.

It is critical to find ways to interrupt offensive humor that puts people or nations down. I choose to be pro-active rather than negative, to listen and learn about humor in other cultures. It is also valuable to learn about other cultures through humor, whether the culture is based on ethnic origin, sexual orientation, or people who are differently abled.

In *Don't Get Me Started*, comedian Kate Clinton writes that "I'm out and proud. When I'm out and it's raining I carry an umbrella. I used to be in but I hate the smell of moth balls. My closet was huge, complete with a foyer, turnstile, a few locks, dead bolts, and a burglar alarm that had to be deactivated before I could even touch the door handle."

In another anecdote, she writes, "Once when my Dad was visiting, he sat through an evening of gay politics, gay theory,

gay gossip, and toward the end of the discussion, my partner turned to him and asked, 'Well, Mr. Clinton, what do you think we as gay people can do to make more bridges to straight people?' My Dad did one of his patented, exquisitely timed pauses and replied, 'Keep talking.'"

"Laughter has no accent."

—Jim Boren (in *Laffirmations*)

Learning about humor in other cultures is an adventure, whether it is through reading, traveling, or shared conversations. Often, when I ask, "What makes you laugh?" people respond with laughter. Sometimes, with folks from a different culture, there is a language barrier or details get lost in the translation. Even though we don't always understand every word, the question is worth asking just to see their faces light up as they recall funny times from the past.

Is there such a thing as the world's funniest joke?

—JoAnn Shroyer, author

Use humor as an opportunity to get to know others. Initiate a conversation about humor and culture. Ask them how their culture expresses or encourages humor.

In my recent travels, I met a young man from Turkey. In our conversation about humor and culture, he recommended the works of Nazreddin, a famous exemplar of Sufi (Muslim mystics). I discovered the following story in a collection of Sufi readings, *Another Way of Laughter* by Massud Farzan.

The Mind Reader: A man was claiming to be God's prophet. He was taken to the Caliph, who said: "Prophets reveal miracles. What is yours?" The man replied: "I have the ability to read thoughts. Right now you are all thinking that I am lying."

In an article, "Indian Humor" in *Race, Class, Gender: An Anthology,* American Indian writer Vine Deloria asserts, "One of the best ways to understand a people is to know what makes them laugh. Laughter encompasses the limits of the soul. In humor, life is redefined and accepted. Irony and satire provide much keener insights into a group's collective psyche and values than do years of research."

Tou Ger Xiong, the first Hmong comedian in the United States, teaches culture through laughter. Through humor, folklore, and hip-hop music, his presentation is a cultural journey for the heart, spirit, and funny bone. "As much as we are different, we are alike in many ways. We have no choice but to get along. . . . When you get someone to laugh, you can talk about anything." [www.gohmongboy.com]

I bought Xiong's video, "I Is Hmong." To my surprise, much of it is spoken in Hmong without translations. Although I couldn't understand the comments, it was worth watching for the audience's response to Xiong's humor.

Honey Hush: An Anthology of African-American Women's Humor, a book by Daryl Cumber Dance, is a delightful way to learn about another culture. Dance writes about how and why African-American women were prevented from sharing their humor in public. She shares the abundance, richness, and soul-saving importance of humor in the homes of African-American women—historically and in the present time. What a gift to her readers!

Humor and Tragedy

Humor has long been a tool for surviving and thriving while dealing with the stress of oppression. Humor can help to create a world that works for everyone. According to comedian Carol Burnett, "Humor is tragedy plus time."

When you consider the amount of time we spend on what is wrong with the world, listening to bad news, we can find ourselves stuck in a paradigm of tragedy. How can we develop the ability to see the comedy within our tragedies sooner than later? How can we participate in furthering the paradigm shift and give equal time to the comedy of our lives?

Our openness to see reality from a new perspective offers us the ability to place ourselves and our lives in a greater context, a context where making a difference is of the utmost importance. People who are able to laugh in the face of hardship, even death, are often the ones who live to tell about it.

Prisoners who overcame the hardships of Nazi-imposed ghettos and apartheid jail cells often attributed their survival to their sense of humor. Laughter is not our only defense against despair, but it can also play a key role in freeing us from the stresses that sap our will to live.

A contemporary example of the ability to see humor under tragic circumstances is in *Veiled Courage: Inside the Afghan Women's Resistance Movement* by Cheryl Benard. *Veiled Courage* highlights the courage of Meena, the martyred founder of the Revolutionary Association of Women of Afghanistan, RAWA. Despite the loud noises in the neighborhood indicating the presence of KHAD, the Afghan secret police, Meena chose to move about one night, carrying on the work of the revolution. The next day she found out what all the commotion in the neighborhood was. Fathana, the wife of the head of the Afghan secret police, was attempting to run away with her lover. To prevent Fathana from running away, the police surrounded the house where she was hiding. Meena laughed and said, "May God keep them busy with each other's strange affairs. Then they won't have time to come after us."

Despite years of suppression, Afghan women find opportunities to laugh. The Taliban forbade women from laughing too loudly—no stranger should hear the voice of a woman, "because this risked sexually exciting males," Benard explained. Taliban law may have been able to quiet some of the laughter, but definitely not all.

If you think you are too small to be effective, you've never been in bed with a mosquito. On 500,000 Web sites

Humor and Justice Role Models

Besides Meena of RAWA and women like her, who are role models, wisdom figures, people who effectively worked for justice and displayed humor? Mother Teresa, the Dali Lama, Mahatma Gandhi, Eleanor Roosevelt, Jesus, and Abraham Lincoln are some of the ones who come to my mind. It is not widely known that Mark Twain was an advocate for social justice.

Mother Teresa: "I know God will not give me anything I can't handle. I just wish that (God) didn't trust me so much."

Gandhi said: "I believe in equality for everyone, except reporters and photographers."

After being accused of being a liar, a cheat and a two-faced politician, Abraham Lincoln responded: "If I were two-faced, would I be wearing this one?"

Eleanor Roosevelt: "Beautiful young people are accidents of nature, but beautiful old people are works of art." "A woman is like a tea bag. You never know how strong she is until she gets in hot water."

Although I don't have a story or quote to represent the humor of the Dalai Lama, anyone who has spent time in his presence, even in an audience of thousands, remembers the happy countenance he radiates. For me, the Dalai Lama represents a leader who effectively educates about suffering, compassion, peace and justice, and, at the same time, projects lightheartedness.

Aside from these international and national role models of humor, there are, undoubtedly, role models and wisdom figures in our own backyard. For example, the late Sister Rose Tillemans of Minneapolis, Minnesota, reminds me of Mother Teresa. Both were feisty nuns who worked with the poorest of the poor. Sister Rose graciously laughed and cried all the while working tirelessly for social justice. She successfully turned her anger and frustration with the system into playful poetry. An example:

> **MY CUP OF TEA**
> **With statements hierarchical**
> **I don't feel very spark-ical.**
> **But I would serve some cups of tea**
> **To members of the hierarchy**
> **And ask a blessing for my home**
> **If they would let me come to Rome**
> **To bless their space with woman's hand**
> **And talk with them of all they've banned.**
>
> —Rose Tillemans, Sisters of St. Joseph
> Reprinted with permission

We seldom appreciate the ways our co-workers, spouses, children, neighbors or even clergy use humor to deal with the everyday upsets of life. Seek to acknowledge them.

People with less power and resources inherently see the world through different lenses from those with the most power. Those with less power often resort to comedy as a safe way of challenging the current unjust paradigm.

Comedian and activist Dick Gregory demonstrated his ability to use humor to challenge racism: "Last time I was down South I walked into this restaurant, and this white waitress came up to me and said: 'We don't serve colored people here.' I said: 'That's all right. I don't eat colored people. Bring me a whole fried chicken.' About that time these three cousins come in, you know the ones I mean, Klu, Kluck, and Klan, and they say: 'Boy, we're givin' you fair warnin'. Anything you do to that chicken, we're gonna do to you.' About then the waitress brought me my chicken. 'Remember, boy, anything you do to that chicken, we're gonna do to you.' So I put down my knife and fork, and I picked up that chicken, and I kissed it." *Nigger*, back cover, Simon and Schuster

An act of self-determination in the face of overwhelming obstacles promotes survival and thriving of the soul, even when we find ourselves in the worst of circumstances.

Another humorous paradigm shift from RAWA is a product sold on the Web: On the one hand, you had the Taliban trying to impose an ultra-Victorian, puritanical order, and on the other, you had the Revolutionary Association of Women of Afghanistan outfitting men in underwear stamped with the socialist-realist image of five combative women raising a banner imprinted with the words, "Freedom, democracy, women's rights." www.rawa.com

I was ridin' along in my Cadillac, you know, goin' through one of them little towns in South Carolina. Pass through a red light. One of them big cops runnin' over to me, say, "Hey, woman, don't you know you went through a red light?" I say, "Yeah, I know I went through a red light." "Well, what did you do

70

that for?" I said, "'Cause I seen all you white folks goin' on the green light . . . thought the red light was for us."

—Moms Mabley from *A Heart Full of Grace: 1000 Years of Black Wisdom*

In Richard Attenborough's 1987 movie, *Cry Freedom*, a South African judge asked Civil Rights activist Stephen Biko, "You people look brown to me. Why do you call yourselves 'Blacks'?" Biko responded, "You people look pink to me. Why do you call yourself white?"

Those of us working for peace and social justice tend to get too serious, which reduces our effectiveness and often results in burnout. It is not easy to maintain a light spirit while working for peace and justice. We must ask ourselves: How can we use laughter and play to thrive, not just survive, as we work for social justice? How can we be more effective in educating people about the issues and, at the same time, enlisting their participation by using humor?

Shifting the Peace Paradigm

"If I can't dance, I don't want to be part of the revolution."

—Emma Goldman, revolutionary activist

I say, "If I can't laugh, I don't want to be part of the transformation."

Besides the individual wisdom figures, what groups and movements demonstrate an effective use of humor in working for peace and justice?

In *In Stitches: A Patchwork of Feminist Humor and Satire*, Gloria Kaufman compares feminist humor with mainstream attack humor. The laughter of a put-down "smears a smile over someone's pain and leaves its victim hurting. . . . The smirk of the superior is not a positive thing."

Feminist humor invites "the powerful" to change their behavior and join the laughter. The intent is to educate rather than damage its object. Too often mainstream humor hurts those with less power and maintains the hierarchy and status quo. The intention of feminist humor is to educate all and stimulate transformation in the direction

71

of peace with justice. Feminist humor "is concerned with the transfer of power from those who have it overwhelmingly to those who have too little."

From *Hi, this is Sylvia* by Nicole Hollander. Used with permission

The use of humor and comedy is one of the safest and most effective ways to challenge the current paradigm without putting ourselves in harm's way. Comedians help people see the irony of their actions.

In *Color Me Flo*, Florynce Kennedy, a feminist, social justice advocate, and one of the first African American women lawyers, playfully pointed out the flaws in the system during a run-in with a judge:

When women began wearing pants there was a tremendous backlash. I can remember—I was still practicing law at that time—going to court in pants and the judge's remarking that I wasn't properly dressed, that the next time I came to court I should be dressed like a lawyer. He's sitting there in a long black dress gathered at the yoke, and I said, "Judge, if you won't talk about what I'm wearing, I won't talk about what you're wearing," because it occurred to me that a judge in a skirt telling me not to wear pants was just a little bit ludicrous. It's interesting to speculate how it developed that in two of the most anti-feminist institutions, the church and the law court, the men are wearing the dresses.

For Flo Kennedy, social activism was not a question of courage or bravery. It was the "cheapest way to have fun."

Humor promotes shifting the protest paradigm: Jessica Misslan noticed a deflation of energy at a rally when a speaker began ranting against the current political policy. That is why she titled her article in *Utne Reader*, "Make Protests Fun: 1-2-3-4, we don't want shrill chants no more." Angry yelling doesn't work. To rant, rave or make people wrong only makes people defensive. There is a Sufi saying: "Out beyond right and wrong there is a field. I will meet you there." Misslan urges us to be more creative and have more fun in our political gatherings—to demonstrate—that is, to practice the peace we preach in our demonstrations. We must demonstrate what we stand for, demonstrate what works and invite others to join.

Code Pink, a playful, passionate political movement, urges us to speak up for what we stand for—to show our true colors. Code Pink calls for serious and playful responses to war, economic collapse, the loss of civil liberties, and environmental disaster. Playful spontaneity and a sense of respect for all sets the Code Pink movement apart from the old-paradigm protest. It seeks to connect people rather than drive them further apart; "time is short and the risks too serious for anything but love," notes Nina Utne in "Think Pink," in the *Utne Reader*.

I have a scheme for stopping war. It's this: no nation is allowed to enter a war until they have paid for the last one.

—Will Rogers, humorist

I want you to hold this vision with me: all of the world leaders at the UN begin their sessions with the Hokey Pokey. What if Ariel Sharon and Yasser Arafat put their whole selves in? That would be commitment. And then pulled their whole selves out. That is detachment. Then they turn themselves around, which is transformation. And that, my friends, is what it is all about.

—Swami Beyondanda, leader of the Laughmore Society

Laughmore Society motto: Overcome with Laughter

www.wakeuplaughing.com

Ideas

- Who are the wisdom figures that inspire you to work for peace and justice? What do you know about their humor? If they are still alive, acknowledge them for being an inspiration and ask them what they do to lighten up.
- Get to know the humor of another culture through conversations, Web searches, and music.
- Have a humor party or salon, inviting people with various backgrounds and cultures to discuss their experience of humor.
- Include humor when celebrating Women's History Month, African-American History Month, and other events for specific ethnic groups. Hold a story hour, inviting people of various cultures to share stories that teach about their culture.
- Collect quotes about humor from other cultures and traditions: Chilean poet Pablo Neruda says, *Humor is the language of the soul.* Hafiz, a fourteenth century Persian poet says, *Laughter is the sun poking its sweet head out from the clouds within. Laughter is a soul waking up!* (translated by Daniel Ladinsky). Consider turning this idea into a contest at your workplace.
- Collect riddles, funny stories, or jokes from other cultures. Share these with children and adults.

Q: Wonder, wonder, what can it be? Born in the woods, it lives on the river. A: A canoe. (Paraguay: Guarani)

Q: If you want to become wise, turn me over on my back and open up my belly. What am I? A: A book! (Iceland)

Q: When does everybody in the world speak the same language? A: When they are babies crying. (Siberia: Yakut) Another Answer: When people are laughing.

Q: Tie him up and he runs, but untie him and he stands still. What is it? A: A shoe. (Tibet)

Q: A great blue bowl filled with popcorn. What is it? A: The sky and stars. (Mexico: Aztec)

Q: Which animal is stronger than all the others? A: The skunk! (America: Comanche)

Q: Just two hairs upon her head, but she wears a flowered gown as she dances along the flower bed. What is she? A: A butterfly! (China)

From *Crazy Gibberish* by Naomi Baltuck

Learn to speak another language and enjoy your own language bloopers. Speaking a foreign language often offers opportunities for humor. While in Nicaragua, I wanted to buy a piece of leather (*cuero*) to make a necklace, instead I asked for a piece of body (*cuerpo*). In Germany, my friend Barbara asked for *zahne* (teeth) in her coffee. She thought she was saying *sahne* (cream).

Since language can be a barrier to humor, my friend Julie connects with people in other countries through body tricks. She is double jointed, and she can make anyone laugh as she raises her leg straight up in front of her body.

My e-mail friend from Ireland, Catherine, shared the story of an unforgettable taxi ride with her sister who is disabled and uses a wheelchair: The taxi driver put the wheelchair in the boot (the trunk) of the car but he couldn't close the door because the wheelchair was too big. When we got home, the wheelchair was missing. My brother walked back on the road where we had traveled and an ambulance, police and lots of people were gathered around. The wheelchair was in the middle of the road. They thought there had been an accident and were hunting for the missing person. My brother tried to take the wheelchair back, but the police wouldn't believe him. Eventually they gave the chair back to my sister. We couldn't stop laughing.

Bumper Sticker: "I love my country but I think we should start seeing other people." Northern Sun Distribution

Gay Pride T-shirt slogan: I can't even think straight.

The only queer people are those who don't love anybody.

—Rita Mae Brown, author

In *Revolutionary Laughter*, comedian **Suzy Berger** states: **"Gay material is a lot like Jewish material. If comedy is good, it's universal. It does translate. I did one line about being lesbian: 'You know that my family always said no man would be good enough for me,' and they (the audience) just lost it. Because don't they all say that to their daughters."**

Clowning. People take up clowning for various reasons—as a spiritual ministry, for healing and entertainment. For Ginger Hedstrom, becoming a clown was part of her process of healing from being a battered woman. She now gives presentations about her recovery as she puts on her clown costume. Blossom the Clown's definition of universal health care is healthy humor that lifts up, cheers up and rises above the troubles of life. It is available to all, no insurance plan necessary.

Ginger adds, "Our global world is composed of a multitude of nationalities, cultures, languages, dialects, diets, and medical practices that are more diverse than can be defined. The gift of healthy humor—spread through smiles and laughter—releases healing endorphins and creates an interruption in the lives of all people."

Blossom the Clown   Photo by Ginger Hedstrom

VI

Spirituality and Humor
And God Created Laughter

Funny
Sometimes laughter erupts
From deep volcanic soul space
Surprising solemn moments like
Blue crocuses in spring snow.
—Nagueyalti Warren, poet
Reprinted with permission

According to an old rabbinic tale, humanity went in search of God, leaving its homeland and climbing a very high mountain, where God could certainly be found. At the same time, the lonely God decided to come down from the mountain to dwell at one with humanity. They missed each other en route, and humanity ever since has been seeking God in those rarefied heights, while God remains present in the ordinary things of the earth.

Mrs. Jones climbed a mountain in search of a guru who lived on one of the highest peaks. After three weeks of travel and great hardship, she finally reached the peak. A young disciple of the guru told her, "The guru is unavailable but can see you in two days, on Tuesday, at two in the morning. In the meantime, you can stay in this hut."

Mrs. Jones stayed in the leaky stick hut for two days. It was cold and wet, and she slept on the ground. She ate nuts, wild

berries, and churned yak milk. On Tuesday, just before two in the morning, the young disciple came to lead her to another hut. There sat the guru. Mrs. Jones went right up to him. She said, "Murray, come home!"

Many of us seldom connect God with humor. "*Genuine humor —the kind that makes people laugh about the human condition—is always a religious experience,*" says comedian Merrilyn Belgum in an interview in *Minnesota Women's Press.* Arthur Schopenhauer, a German philosopher, stated that "*a sense of humor is the only divine quality of man.*"

The intention of this section is to explore the relationship between spirituality and humor in such a way that we more fully embrace our humanity and the spark of divinity within. People, according to Lynne Twist in *The Soul of Money,* "want an experience of their own divinity, their own connectedness with all life and the mystery of something greater than we comprehend."

The spiritual life has four qualities: common sense, common sense, common sense, and a sense of humor.   Source unknown

Although my heritage is Christian, I am not promoting a particular path or set of beliefs. I am encouraging an exploration of the relationship between spirituality and humor, an exploration of our relationship with the God of our understanding.

I asked Sister Arlene Hynes, O.S.B., about the relationship between spirituality and humor. She said, "It's the difference between heaven and hell."

I asked her how she knew that. She replied with a gleam in her eyes, "I'm Irish."

A God of Humor

Two guys have been debating for years whether God is black or white. While on a fishing trip together, they are killed in an accident. While waiting outside the Pearly Gates, they are still

arguing about whether God is black or white. Then it dawns on them that they will get their answer. They call Peter over to ask the big question. Before Peter could answer, God walks up. She says, "Buenos dias, Señores." On over 500 Web sites

Joan Timmerman, theologian and author, refers to spirituality as "a conversation, sometimes interrupted, sometimes lively, but always ongoing with that Unknown with which the known is connected." It is a holistic response: mind, body, spirit—to our perception of the Unknown, the Great Mystery. We seek the connection to the Unknown in many areas of life—music, art, work, prayer, nature, relationships, and humor.

In *Letters to a Young Poet*, Rainer Maria Rilke says: *"Be patient toward all that is unresolved in your heart and try to love the questions themselves like locked rooms and like books written in a foreign tongue. . . . Live the questions now."*

What is our response to that Unknown with which the known is connected? What does our experience of humor reveal about who God is? How can humor call forth the magnificence of the human spirit? These are questions I am learning to live.

When we take ourselves too seriously, there is no room for the magnificence of the human spirit to shine forth. The Tibetans have a saying: *Humor creates space where there is none.* I like to think they are referring to space for awe, joy, and wonderment.

I have discovered that my sense of humor expands in direct proportion to the expansion of my notion of God and vice versa. When I lose my sense of humor, my conversation with God is blocked. I am not open. I stop listening for the still, small voice within. When my sense of humor is alive, I am open to spiritual growth.

Several years ago, I realized I was still operating from my childhood image of God. Even though I may have heard words like "merciful" and "compassionate," He was unfriendly, unapproachable. God as the old, white male judge in the sky was the predominant picture in my head. Like Santa Claus, God was waiting to catch me being bad. I participated in a Twelve-Step group Al-Anon for several years before I actually heard the word "care" in the third step: Made a decision to turn our will and our lives over to the *care* of God, as we understand God.

At that point, I also realized I was not letting in the care of others. A co-worker, Bruce, mentioned that he had not seen me around lately. Prior to my awakening to a caring God, I would have heard his comment as condemnation: Where have you been? You should be around more. This time I was able to let in the care. I heard that he missed me.

My awareness helped me let go of that limited and limiting impression of God. I was then open to another spiritual awakening. I heard the still, small voice within telling me that "I am in God and God is in me." This healing experience gave me a greater sense of wholeness and freedom to laugh and enjoy life.

Recently, my spiritual director asked me how my work on this book has affected my relationship with God. Investing myself in this book required tremendous trust. The process required that I trust and accept the contribution of others—reading, criticizing, editing and encouraging me along the way. It is fitting that I acknowledge a dozen others. It has been an experience of God as love and trust. No wonder relational trust is a major theme of the book.

What is your understanding of God, Allah, Yahweh, Buddha, the Great Spirit, the Presence, the Other, the Divine? What images and experiences of God give you freedom to laugh and enjoy life to its fullest? Theologian Thomas Merton preferred the name Mercy. He wrote, "God is like a calm sea of mercy." For those raised with the notion of a God as judge, the image of God as Mercy can be a refreshing source of light and joy. Merton describes prayer as "the response of God within us, the discovery of God within us."

Jesus Laughing

Ralph Kozak, Praise Prints   Used with permission

80

In *I'm Still Dancing*, Sister Rose Tillemans imagined a God of fun and laughter. She writes, "Fun, foolishness, and frolic are sacraments for me, though they are not listed in the catechism. Thank you, god of Laughter, for such blessings."

Alice Walker's well-known conversation about God in *The Color Purple* is my favorite. Shug tells Celie:

> My first step from the old white man was trees. Then air. Then birds. Then other people. But one day when I was sitting quiet and feeling like a motherless child, which I was, it come to me: that feeling of being part of everything, not separate at all. I knew that if I cut a tree, my arm would bleed. And I laughed and cried and I run all round the house. I knew just what it was. In fact, when it happen, you can't miss it. It sort of like you know what, she say, grinning and rubbing high up on my thigh.

Talk about an image that evokes the freedom to laugh and enjoy life: the trees, air, birds, "you know what," and love!

When expanding your image of God, be prepared for surprises. At the start of an eight-day silent retreat, my spiritual director, a seventy-year-old Jesuit priest, encouraged me to "be on vacation with God." When I met with him for spiritual direction the next day, I mentioned that my vacation had turned into a honeymoon. I had had an erotic dream that first night!

In *The Unknown She*, Andrew Harvey states, "If you really open your heart to the possibility of a direct encounter with the divine, what you'll discover very, very fast is that the divine has nothing to do with all these rules and regulations and glooms and despairs. The divine is here, in life, in the world as rapture and the fire of eternal joy."

Our images and ideas tell us more about us than about God. If you do not believe God has a sense of humor, look in the mirror. No image, concept or idea can adequately express who God is. God always remains the Great Mystery. Every once in a while we get a tiny glimpse, an inkling of the Unimaginable, the Inexpressible.

Although I don't have it all sorted out, I am convinced there is a connection between our ability to laugh and play and our being comfortable with and accepting of mystery in our lives. Many of us get impatient and want to know the answers, to read "the last page" without experiencing the whole mystery.

The good news is that there are many lighthearted messages about laughter and joy in the various world religions. The bad news is that heavy theological tomes often overshadow these messages.

I encourage you to take another look at your religious tradition, digging deeper for the joyful news. In addition to searching my own tradition, I enjoy seeking out the positive messages from other traditions.

Laughing Buddha, drawing by Spikey

The Koran, the Islamic holy book, states, *"Those who make their companions laugh deserve paradise."* The Talmud, a Jewish holy book, says, *"People will be called to account on Judgment Day for every permissible thing they might have enjoyed but did not."* Andrew Harvey, who was born in India, offers: *"Temples are fun; priests are fun with their gold robes and the sweets they give you. And Indians have hilarious sacred holidays like Holi where they rush around and shriek and fling paint on everything. And the actual gods are fun. It's great to have an elephant god! Hinduism has at its core hilarity, a joi de vivre, a phenomenal acceptance of the gaiety of the human world."* Rumi: *"Everything that you love and enjoy is a ray from the sun of the Beloved."*

A creation story in the lore of the Apache Indians tells about how the Creator was delighted in making the first humans able to do so many things. They could see, hear, talk, run, dance, and create things with their hands. However, God wasn't fully satisfied. Something seemed to be lacking in these wonderful new beings. Therefore, the

Creator went back to the creation studio and experimented with different possibilities. At long last, the one final thing that was needed became clear: it was laughter! And when the first humans were given this essential, new gift, they laughed and laughed. It was only on hearing this that the Creator said, "Now you are fit to live."

In the Navajo nation, laughter is a sign of holiness. "The holy people in our community, the ones we turned to for spiritual guidance and who conducted the blessing and healing ceremonies, were always the people who had the keenest sense of humor. You could spot them by the laugh wrinkles near their eyes. . . . The hallmark of holiness was . . . a common lively sense of humor, honed from birth on the lathe of life's ups and downs, its absurdities and sorrows, its joys and unpredictable encounters. Humor is a side effect of living deeply. . . ."

From "Spirit in a World of Connection" by Rich Heffern
National Catholic Reporter (NCR)

There is a direct relationship between growing spiritually, our ability to be with the mystery of life, and developing our sense of humor. Sister Renee Domeier, O.S.B., raises more questions to learn to live: Is it our image of God that gives us our permission or ability to laugh? Or might it be our innate, initial delight in such things as the incongruous, our expecting the unexpected, and our humility before the mystery of it all? And then, that may change our image of God.

I'm a godmother, that's a great thing to be. She calls me god for short, that's cute. I taught her that. —Ellen DeGeneres, comedian

From *Children's Letters to God*

Dear GOD, I read the Bible. What does "begat" mean? Nobody will tell me. Love —Alison

Dear GOD, How did you know you were God? Who told you? —Charlene

Dear GOD, Are you really invisible or is it just a trick? —Lucy

Dear GOD, My brother told me about being born but it doesn't sound right. He's just kidding, isn't he?

—**Marsha**

Dear GOD, I didn't think orange went with purple until I saw the sunset you made on Tuesday. That was cool.

—**Eugene**

Ideas

Start a new tradition. After a Navajo baby is born, the first celebration takes place just after the child's first laugh. Yes, laugh! "We believe the soul (also called 'the wind') enters the body soon after birth," says Lori Alviso Alvord, a Navajo physician. "A baby's laugh is an indication that the soul has become attached to the body."   *NCR*

Give a halo as a gift of humor. My friend Barbara gave me a halo head band. While wearing it, I get a laugh when I tell people that "I am holier than thou." Now I am looking for angel wings to attach to the seat of my slacks. So often it seems that I'm "flying by the seat of my pants."

Caricatures by Spikey

84

Spirituality and Humor

Play with Spontaneity

Although there are many reasons we are not spontaneous, our religious tradition may have encouraged or discouraged it. Playing with spontaneity is another way to promote laughter. I never thought of myself as spontaneous, but lately, I've had fun practicing being more self-expressed. Instead of always censoring myself, I have had more spontaneous exchanges with people.

For example, one cool, spring morning I was out for a walk. A woman walking in front of me had one hand up her sleeve. I thought, "I wonder if she knows she is missing a hand?" Then I remembered that I had one hand clapper (the little plastic toy in the shape of a hand) in my pocket. I walked up to her. When I saw the smile of greeting on her face, I knew it was okay to say to her, "You seem to be missing a hand. I happen to have an extra." She laughed and took the hand. It was a bonding experience.

85

VII

Laugh, Reduce Stress and Heal

Norman Cousins made the healing power of humor famous in his groundbreaking book, *The Anatomy of an Illness*. While suffering from a very painful, life-threatening spinal disease, Cousins discovered that with every ten minutes of hearty laughter, he could sleep pain-free for two hours. Watching Laurel and Hardy, the Marx Brothers, and old Candid Camera reruns made him laugh. Cousins was crafting his "humor survival kit." Isn't it funny, we spend more time making arrangements for our last will and testament than creating our own humor survival kits.

After Cousins' experience became known, several physicians shared his writing with patients whose will to live needed a boost. Occasionally they asked Cousins to telephone their patients. He relates the story of one young woman, Carole, who was gradually losing the use of her legs. Her entire family was becoming unhinged by worry and despair. She needed to know if Norman was ever discouraged during his devastating illness. He replied,

> . . . especially at the start when I expected my doctors to fix my body as though it were an automobile engine that needed mechanical repair, like cleaning out the carburetor, or reconnecting the fuel pump. But then I realized that a human being is not a machine—and only a human being has a built-in mechanism for repairing itself, for ministering to its own needs, and for comprehending what is happening to it. The

regenerative and restorative force in human beings is at the core of human uniqueness.

Carole's doctor gave her good advice when he told her that his treatment would work best when combined with the natural drive of the body to restore itself.

Family members took turns going to the library in order to find books with genuine laugh-producing qualities. Cousins asked Carole to call him at 9:30 A.M. each day to share a story. What a phenomenal treasure hunt! The quality of life for the whole family improved.

Once again, we hear the theme of relational trust, this time in terms of trusting our bodies and healthcare professionals. In order to tap into the healing power of humor, we need an underlying faith and confidence in the natural drive of the body to regenerate itself.

One of the keys to Cousins' recovery was the recognition of the restorative ability of the human body and his active participation in the healing process. He created a powerful partnership with his doctors. As we grow to understand and trust our bodies and become more effective in creating partnerships with health professionals, we will be more effective in tapping into the healing power of humor.

> There is no dirth
> Of healthy mirth.
> In fact, humor reduces girth
> And heals the earth.
> —Linda Hutchinson, *ha!*

That poem illuminates two vital benefits of humor: promoting healing and providing physical exercise. A wise friend, now in her seventh decade, asserts that humor can heal the earth. When you think about it, plant lovers talk to their plants. Why not laugh to heal the earth? I believe laughing, in some mysterious but profound way, does heal the earth. In *Selected Poems* by Langston Hughes, he writes, "Like a welcome summer rain, humor may suddenly cleanse and cool the earth, the air and you."

Regarding the humor and girth relationship, Dr. William Fry, a Stanford professor of psychiatry, studied laughter for over thirty years, concluding that the physical effects of laughter parallel the benefits of physical exercise. In the mind's eye, hearty laughter is like internal jogging. When laughing, we burn up to seventy-five more calories than while resting. Guffaws, I'm sure, are good for a few extra calories.

As I lighten up, I lighten up. —Linda Hutchinson, *ha!*

The old man laughed joyously and loud, shook up the details of his anatomy from head to foot, saying that such a laugh was money in a man's pocket because it cut down on the doctor's bills like everything.
—Mark Twain, humorist

The connection between humor and health is not a new concept. During the Middle Ages the word "humor" referred to the four fluids of the body: blood, phlegm, choler, and black bile. The ancient physiologists believed that the relative proportions of these fluids determined a person's disposition and general health. Perhaps they were onto something. Our sense of humor definitely makes a difference in our disposition and general health. The health industry has been a leader in calling forth the healing power of humor.

Humor is:
• a tool for the prevention of "dis-ease" and promotion of health and wholeness,
• a diagnostic tool,
• an aid for increasing the effectiveness of treatment and the restoration of well-being.

There is a growing body of research supporting the connection between laughter and health. Dr. William Fry, Dr. Lee Berk at Loma Linda University and Dr. Robert Provine at University of Maryland are known for their research on the healing power of laughter. Within the subject of humor, more is written about humor and health than any other area of life. Research indicates that laughter strengthens the immune system. As an aerobic exercise, it prevents heart disease. It alleviates bronchitis and asthma, assists in the control of blood pressure and prevents depression, anxiety and psychosomatic disorders.

Laughter is a natural painkiller. In the *World Laughter Tour* newsletter, an Australian woman, Sarah Bruhn, describes the pain-killing effects of laughter during pregnancy and labor for her mother and for herself.

My mother had her last child three years ago, and during her labour I was present. I was stunned to find my mother in the last part of labour laughing in the brief moments between contractions. Her labour was quick with no interference, and she had an unusually quick recovery. She also made a point of laughing every day during her pregnancy. She told me she had done the same with both of her other children (including me) instinctively, and the outcome was always the same: healthy mother and baby. Last year I had my first child and did the same thing, laughed through pregnancy and labour. Since I was just sixteen, my midwife was surprised at how quick and relatively easy my labour was compared to other mothers who were older than I and even had had more than one child.

Put laughter on the menu if you have diabetes. According to a Japanese study reported in *Diabetes Care*, laughing can lower your blood sugar. Positive emotions such as laughter may control spikes in blood sugar levels after a meal. People with diabetes who watched a funny video during dinner had lower blood sugar levels after the meal compared to the people who watched a lecture video.

Be happy and don't worry about getting a cold! *Psychosomatic Medicine* reports a research study by Sheldon Cohen, professor of psychology at Carnegie Mellon University in Pittsburgh. He found that people who are more positive—more often happy and calm—are less likely to develop colds than people who are gloomy.

Laughter really is the best medicine. Even the Judeo-Christian Scriptures instruct us to reflect on the relationship between humor and health: *A cheerful or merry heart is good medicine.* (Proverbs 17:22)

Stress

Laughter is one of the most effective tools we have in over-coming stress and the limitations it puts on our lives. Humor allows us to forego pomposity, and increases our possibilities to discover options and live joyfully.

—Loretta LaRoche, public speaker

Stress is one of the leading causes of ill health. Humor, a powerful coping mechanism, relieves stress and adds years to life. The Loma Linda University Web site states that, according to a President's Science Advisory, stress costs our economy $200 billion annually.

According to Jane Wagner, in her delightful book, *The Search for Signs of Intelligent Life in the Universe,* "Reality is the greatest source of stress amongst those in touch with it." Wagner further asserts that since she put reality on the "back burner," her life became "jam-packed and fun-filled." One way of reducing tension in our lives is to envision a lighter view of reality. For instance, I grew up with the notion that life is hard work. Since I have now put that view of reality on the back burner, my life, too, has become jam-packed and fun-filled.

In my humor workshops, we explore various uses of humor to turn tense situations around and brainstorm lighthearted options for reducing the impact of stress on our lives. Stress is one component of life, perhaps, part of the human condition. Stress emanates from positive events as well as negative. Whatever the source, we can learn to reduce its impact in our lives by incorporating laughter into our day. One common source of stress, particularly for women, is taking someone's comments too seriously. It is not easy, but since I've applied the practice of not being offended, I am a lot happier and more serene. People

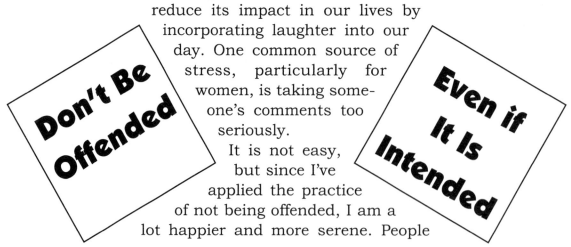

Don't Put Up with Put-downs

have to work harder to offend me. On the other hand, it's a paradox. Don't be offended, and don't put up with put-downs. I urge people who are offended by toxic humor to use the offense as an opportunity to educate.

One simple technique is to ask the offender to explain the joke or comment. A joke often loses its appeal when it needs to be explained. Avoid sources of negative humor. That is, avoid people you experience as being negative or offensive. Another way to build your humor immunity is to be prepared. Who says humor always has to be spontaneous? Have humorous comebacks ready for situations or circumstances that repeatedly happen.

In her book, *They Used to Call Me Snow White But I Drifted: Women's Strategic Use of Humor*, Regina Barreca describes a great comeback. Former news anchor Connie Chung was asked by a new co-worker about the relationship between her position as an Asian-American woman and her rapid rise in the broadcasting field. Her response to the insensitive question was both keen and humorous. She pointed to the senior vice president and announced, "Bill likes the way I do his shirts."

Personally, I am not quick at comebacks. I often think of a funny response to a situation a day or two later. Of course, it's better late than never. It takes practice. I still enjoy my funny responses even if they don't occur to me right away. At times when you wished that you had a witty response, talk it over with others. Together you might come up with one. Even if you didn't get to use it at the moment, it can be a good way to let go of negative experiences. And you'll be prepared if a similar situation happens again.

During one humor and spirituality retreat, a participant, Pam, brought up the following situation in which she would have liked a comeback: While she was standing in a buffet line at a restaurant, a couple of white guys behind her were impatient with two Latinos ahead of them and snidely questioned whether the Latinos had green cards. Her response might have been to say, "I wonder where we would be if Native Americans had required us to have green cards."

Humor as Aikido or "Tongue-Fu"

For many of us, fighting or fleeing is the automatic reaction to conflict. It is possible to develop a third way—go with the flow. Thomas Crum, author of *The Magic of Conflict*, teaches the martial art aikido as a metaphor for embracing conflict as an opportunity. Rather than fighting back or running away, you learn to go with the flow, to embrace the energy. Crum urges us to relate to conflict as a gift of energy, in which neither side loses and a new dance is created.

I first encountered Crum at a conference sponsored by The Humor Project in Saratoga Springs, New York. In demonstrating aikido, he proposed that humor can be a verbal form of aikido. Crum tells how a teacher dealt with her students when they all conspired to push their books off their desks at the same time. She had her back to them, writing on the blackboard, when the clock struck 2:00 and in unison the books hit the floor. Without missing a beat, the teacher turned around, pushed her book off her desk, and said, "Sorry I'm late." By joining in the mischief, she demonstrated going with the flow.

Another example of using humor as aikido or "tongue-fu" is from Joel Goodman, director of The Humor Project. He tells the story of a woman who got an obscene phone call at 3:00 A.M. The voice on the other end of the line asked, "Can I take your clothes off?" The woman yelled into the phone, "Well, what the hell are you doing with them on anyway?"

I shared the above stories with the late Bea Swanson, an Ojibwe elder. She said when she gets an obscene phone call, she asks the caller if he needs to talk. She is there to listen.

Some time ago, for my professional growth, I attended a week-long humor workshop in the New York Adirondacks, put on by The Humor

Project. One evening a group of us, men and women, went to the local bar. Usually I don't like the bar scene, but I figured there was safety in numbers. I was standing with our group, when one of the locals, who was drunk, took me by the hand and led me over to dance with his buddy. Mind you, he didn't ask, but just pulled me over. I was shocked and didn't offer resistance at the time. Thank God, his buddy wasn't interested in dancing. A while later when I was sitting at the end of our booth, the same guy came over, picked me up (and I am no featherweight) and carried me to the dance floor to dance with him this time.

The irony was that we had just learned about using humor as aikido. The session was on how humor, like aikido, can be an art form turning a conflicting situation into an opportunity. One learns to use the energy of an attacker and turn the attack into a dance, where no one gets hurt.

Here I am on the dance floor (again without being asked). How do I turn this energy, which feels like an attack, into a dance? It was a fast dance so I could keep my distance from him. However, at one point in the dance, he decided to pick me up again. This time, since I was ready and had my arms in front of me, I pushed off his chest. He finally got the message, and I returned to the booth with the other workshop participants.

I was upset. The next day, for the first time, I had the courage to talk to four men about that experience. I received a broad range of responses. The lawyer said, "Boys will be boys." The psychologist's comment about the man's behavior was that it was inappropriate. The high school counselor realized he had not talked with his eighteen-year-old daughter about these kinds of things. (I appreciated that someone might benefit from this incident.) Finally, the male kindergarten teacher said, "That was a violation." His response made a difference; somebody got it!

At the gift center at the local park, I bought myself a present to turn this negative experience around: a T-shirt with wild animals on it and the inscription—Get to Know the Locals. Despite this experience, it was a wonderful week.

If you want world peace, you must learn to let go of attachments and truly live like nomads. That's where I no mad at you, you no mad at me. —Swami Beyondananda www.WakeUpLaughing.com

In *Laughing All the Way to the Bank* published in the *Minnesota Women's Press*, Pamela Docken described turning embarrassment into success by becoming a comedian. As a short, insecure and dyslexic first-grader, she dreaded being called to the blackboard. Letters and numbers danced in front of her eyes. She sweated and struggled against the tears and her classmates' laughter. She couldn't make them stop laughing. However, she did turn the situation around by pretending she wanted them to laugh. She wasn't failing; she was entertaining. Docken turned her ability to make people laugh into a successful business. In 1999, she opened Oops Theatre in North St. Paul. In only four years, ticket sales passed the million-dollar mark.

Another example of the ability to lighten up a stressful situation involves a group of office workers climbing down the stairs of the World Trade Center Towers on September 11, 2001. They were exhausted by the time they got to the eleventh floor. Someone suggested pretending that it was New Year's Eve and doing a countdown at each floor - 10 - 9 - 8 - 7 - 6 - 5 - 4 - 3 - 2 -1. [From several Web sites]

Laughter Clubs

An exciting development in the world of humor is Laughter Clubs, first launched in 1995 by Dr. Madan Kataria of India. My laughing friend, Norma, and I decided to escape the freezing Minnesota winter and fly to Florida to become certified Laughter Club leaders. Although I had researched Laughter Clubs, I was not convinced that they were for me. My reservations lifted after just a few Laughter Club sessions. It is an absolute hoot!

While writing about the healing power of humor, Kataria decided to create a practical application to his hypothesis. Since people often exercise in the public parks in India, Kataria used the parks as his humor venue. For the first few weeks, the people who came together for laughing told jokes. As time went by, the jokes got worse and the laughter diminished. At that point, Kataria tried another approach and developed a laughter club model with regularly scheduled fifteen- to thirty-minute sessions, which included a variety of laughing exercises, deep breathing, stretching, along with brief discussions of sensible and healthy living. It worked. In four years, the humor movement grew to include over 400 Laughter Clubs and spread throughout the world.

After visiting Dr. Kataria in India in 1998, psychologist Steve Wilson introduced a U.S. version of Laughter Clubs with the World Laughter Tour (WLT). WLT trains and certifies Laughter Club leaders. Leaders learn to establish a sense of safety and relatedness among the participants. It is essential that each person willingly chooses to participate. The WLT mission is to lead the world to health, happiness, and peace through laughter. The motto is Think Globally, Laugh Locally.

Kataria describes the Laughter Club concept and humor movement in his book, *Laughter for No Reason*. This form of "ha-ha yoga," technically called *Hasya yoga*, links breathing exercises with the sounds of laughter. We don't laugh at anything in particular; we laugh for the joy of laughing. The idea is to build on the contagiousness of laughter—to simulate until you stimulate. Soon participants are laughing from the heart, stomach, and toes. We begin with the Laughter Club chant, a succession of hearty Ho, ho, ha, ha, ha! Ho, ho, ha, ha, ha's! Deep breathing to improve the lung capacity follows thirty seconds of all-out hilarity.

There are varieties of invented laughs such as the Silent Laugh. This exercise is reminiscent of all the times we attempted to suppress the giggles. There is also the Lion Laugh, which emulates the lion yoga posture and adds laughter when you stick out your tongue, open your eyes the widest wide and laugh, all at the same time. The Aloha-ha-ha-ha Greeting adds the laughing ha's to the traditional Hawaiian greeting while giving high-fives to fellow laughers. With the Roller Coaster Laugh, you fling your arms up and down while chuckling in rolling waves. The traditional Indian "Namaste" Laughter Greeting includes a bow and a laugh while honoring the spirit in each other. Namaste means recognizing the spirit in each of us. Laughter Club leaders, children, and other good laughers create new exercises every day.

Laughter Clubs provide a mind-body-spirit program, promoting physical health, clear minds and soul-sustaining living. WLT developed a day-by-day model called "Good Hearted Living" that promotes mindfulness and provides a positive focus for each day of the week.

Mondays are for Compliments
Tuesdays are for Flexibility
Wednesdays are for Gratitude
Thursdays are for Kindness
Fridays are for Forgiveness
The weekends are for CHOCOLATE

The Laughter Club movement continues to swell in numbers. There are over 1,000 Laughter Clubs throughout the world. For more WLT information, go to www.worldlaughtertour.com.

Norma and I have offered several laughter classes at the Benedictine monastery. The sisters were lively, engaged and appreciative participants. When we conducted a session for the college library staff, of which Norma is a part, she invented a "Librarian Laugh"—with the index finger across the lips, you repeat "Ha! Ha! Ha! Sh! Sh!"

We have a blast conducting laughter classes and simply taking laughter breaks as needed. When I got too serious while writing this book, I could count on Norma for a spontaneous laughter break. She assists me in practicing what I preach.

My laughter buddy, Jesse, age one   Family photo

I've begun to incorporate laughter sessions in "serious" training. For example, after conducting a staff training program for managers of a medical center, I offered a laughter session based on the Laughter Club model. They all voluntarily chose to participate. Afterward, one of the participants initiated a laughter class with her year-old baby, Drew. When Liz started laughing, Drew readily joined in. What a great role model! We should all have easy, readily available laughter buddies.

There are 900 certified laughter leaders in the United States. Laughter Clubs seem to be especially popular in schools and nursing homes. Recognizing the need to reduce stress in children's lives, some schools offer regular laughter assemblies. The children are free to express goofy laughs and are encouraged to invent new ways of laughing. Picture hundreds of youngsters transforming chirps, meows, woofs and caterwauls into laughter exercises.

I am pleasantly surprised by how much I enjoy laughter sessions and how rewarding it is to lead them. It has loosened me up to laugh more often. It is a good lab for learning about laughter.

Ideas

Give the gift of humor. A humor basket works for a variety of occasions. My friend, Judy, has cancer. I know what makes her laugh. In her humor basket, I put a Jane Wagner *Edith Ann* book, a video of baby animal antics, a couple of wind-up toys, a few copies of the Sunday funnies, and a stuffed animal. She could enjoy these items when she felt like it.

What would you want to receive in a humor basket? Give it to yourself or ask for what you want. My basket includes: *The Search for Signs of Intelligent Life in the Universe* by Jane Wagner (book and video); Calvin and Hobbes cartoon books (my son has the whole collection); wind-up toys (I have at least one hundred); the rubber thing I squeeze and the nose, eyes and ears pop out; an e-mail of a toddler laughing; and the phone numbers of my funniest friends.

Go to the humor section in a bookstore to find gifts. Often there is a good selection on humor, especially for pet lovers. And you don't have to spend a lot of money. Save the Sunday funnies. When someone is not feeling well, give them a packet of funnies to enjoy. Wrap the funnies in nice wrapping paper with a fancy bow.

Stress on the road: If you're laughing, chances are you won't be prone to road rage:
• Keep fun props in the car—like the red nose, groucho glasses or other funny glasses. Use them as needed.
• Look for humor along the way—billboards, license plates, business or bumper stickers that make you laugh.

One billboard read: Be the person your dog thinks you are.

Business: Amigone Funeral Home

Seen on *Funniest Home Videos*

- Listen to upbeat music or story tapes by comedians like Ray Romano, Gilda Radner, or Jay Leno.

I remember listening to Romano's autobiography. He had a couple of tips for staying awake while driving long distances. He would make up sentences that have never been said before such as: Give me back my fudge suitcase. Then he would determine where it might be said: the airport in Hershey Park, Pennsylvania. His second idea, take off all your clothes, may not keep you alert but will surely keep you from falling asleep.

Clothes make the man. Naked people have little or no influence.

Humor therapy is one way to lighten up about something we take too seriously. Humor therapist, Annette Goodheart, recommends that you say out loud something that you take too seriously and at the end say: "Tee Hee!" or "Ha Ha!" I remember seeing her presentation at a humor conference. She invited audience participation. One guy described how he worried a lot and most of what he worried about didn't happen. Goodheart asked him to repeat that and say, "Tee Hee!" It was amazing to see the change. He was so serious about his worries and would crack up when saying, "Tee Hee!" By crack up, I mean laugh "heartily."

In an article in *Eating Disorders: New Directions in Treatment and Recovery*, Sarita Broden uses humor to treat eating disorders. She says that when humor is used by a skilled practitioner, it can "help patients gain an objective view of their behavior, point out the self-damaging effects of black-and-white thinking, debunk some of their myths and distortions and, most of all, cement the therapeutic alliance."

Broden tells of a story, communicated by a client, Karen, in an adolescent/young adult group therapy session: Karen's

98

mother, on the pretext of helping her straighten out her closet, had found several near-empty boxes of laxatives Karen had been using for several weeks. "Wow! You should have seen her!" Karen said. "If you thought she used to get angry at me before, that was nothing! This time the shit really hit the fan!"

Humor is when the joke is on you but hits the other fellow first —because it boomerangs. Humor is what you wish in your secret heart was not funny, but it is, and you must laugh. Humor is your unconscious therapy.
—Langston Hughes, poet, author

If the world didn't suck, we would all fall off.

If at first you don't succeed, skydiving is not for you.

Stupidity is not a handicap. Park elsewhere.

Daily Moment of Zen: Do not walk behind me, for I may not lead. Do not walk ahead of me, for I may not follow. Do not walk beside me either. Just leave me alone.
On 300 Web sites

Change can be one of the greatest sources of stress. I heard this story while on a retreat on contemplation. The retreat was memorable for me because the facilitator included many contemplative jokes. During all the great changes after the Vatican II Council, one religious order did not give the sisters an opportunity to choose between the religious habit and street clothes. They were given dresses and told to come to breakfast the next morning in their new clothes. One older sister did not show up for breakfast. Another sister went to check on the older sister. Sitting on her bed looking out the window, she said, "It's times like these I wish I had said 'Yes' to George."

Humor Collection: Save the humorous cards people send. Create a special cardholder. Share your collection when a friend isn't feeling well.

I have a valentine from thirty years ago. The front of the card says: "The other day someone asked me if you were unattached."

Inside the card reads: "I told them you were just put together kinda funny."

Begin a collection of humorous books or magazine articles or books about humor. My family and friends send me articles about humor published in their local newspapers and magazines.

Program your computer to give you reminders to sit up straight, take a humor break or laugh aloud.

Logo for World Laughter Tour, the people who train Laughter Club leaders

VIII

Laugh, Learn and Create

Humor must not professedly teach and it must not professedly preach, but it must do both if it would live forever.
—Mark Twain, humorist

Mr. B, a great teacher, had an awesome ability to "pick on people" in a playful, loving way. Jimmy, who was in a wheelchair in Mr. B's electronics class, asked Mr. B why he never picked on him. Mr. B was saddened to realize that he was, indeed, not including Jimmy in his playful jibes. As usual, Jimmy wheeled into class late the next day after maneuvering his chair through the crowds of students in the hall. Mr. B began loudly berating Jimmy, saying his chair story was just a lame excuse for a bad attitude. Jimmy's classmates were horrified at Mr. B's tirade—until they saw the look on Jimmy's face. He was beaming. He belonged.

Once again, relational trust is the key to the effective use of humor in learning as well as in teaching. Relational trust is also the key to successful schools. With regard to the story above, teasing is tricky business, but it worked for Mr. B because the students knew that he respected them. Mutual respect was present in that classroom. Not everyone could pull off teasing as well as Mr. B. In fact, teasing is controversial. Some will tell you that there is no place for teasing in the world, that it leads to bullying. I don't agree. As with every other form of humor, it depends on the relationship between the joker and the *jokee*, the teaser and the *teasee*.

What does humor have to do with learning? The original Latin meaning of the word "study" has to do with "zeal"—having an enthusiasm for learning. What has happened to our zeal for learning and our zeal for teaching? This book on humor is an example of my zeal for learning more about humor.

I continue to be delighted and amazed at the books combining humor and other subjects: humor and math, anthropology, music, philosophy, history, literature, psychology, sociology, art, theology, science and nursing. Any subject can be taught or learned with humor. Have fun filling in the gaps of your own education by combining the "missing" subject with humor.

One of my few regrets is that I have never had a music appreciation course. Recently I began exploring music using humor. I discovered that the world-renowned composer and conductor Leonard Bernstein delivered a series of educational programs for young people in the 1960s, which are available on video. I, of course, chose the session on humor in music. He and his orchestra demonstrate various types of humor in music, such as music that is amusing by imitating sounds in nature: a mosquito, rooster, or sneeze. I learned that Haydn's Eighty-eighth Symphony is witty and full of surprises with its sudden changes in speed and loudness. Prokofieff demonstrates satire in music. Because of my lack of music education, I did not always get the humor. However, the program piqued my interest. Now I intend to watch the whole series and to listen to the symphonies that demonstrate humor.

A book of humorous quotes and stories from famous conductors, *The Wit of Music* by Leslie Ayre, includes: A great diva was told that she made more money singing than the President of the United States. She said, "Well, why doesn't he sing then?"

When I searched the Web for music and humor, I discovered a Web site devoted to jokes about instruments. It seems the viola is the butt of many instrument jokes.

How do you keep your violin from getting stolen?
Put it in a viola case.

We all know that a viola is better than a violin because it burns longer. But why does it burn longer?
It's usually still in the case.

Humor makes a positive difference in our ability to learn and teach. Some benefits include:
- increasing retention of subject matter
- enhancing creativity
- energizing the class
- managing anxiety

A hearty laugh gets the endorphins pulsing through our brains, opening our minds to learning or teaching.

It is a myth that no learning occurs if students are laughing. Sometimes teachers fear losing control of their class if laughter is encouraged. Another fear is that the students or administrators will not take them seriously. I have experienced that fear myself. Students acknowledge that laughter and play make a difference in their ability to learn and participate in class.

Laughing together in a classroom or at a conference sets the stage for creating a community of learners. When we laugh together, it reduces our fear of making a mistake or asking a stupid question in front of each other. The statement that the only stupid question is the one you didn't ask is more believable when you have experienced the freedom of laughing together. It also creates a cooperative learning environment.

Ask teachers to share the funny things students have said in their classroom or written in their papers.

Exam Bloopers: A student in a science class wrote, "The universe is a giant orgasm." At the end of the student's essay, the teacher wrote, "Your answer gives new meaning to the Big Bang Theory."

All animals were here before mankind. The animals lived peacefully until mankind came along and made roads, houses, hotels, and condoms.

Involuntary muscles are not as willing as voluntary ones.

When you breathe, you inspire. When you do not breathe, you expire.

Mushrooms always grow in damp places and so they look like umbrellas.

A teacher was teaching about double negatives, when a student asked: Is there such a thing as a double positive? She said, "No." A student from the back of the room piped up, "Yeah, right."

Everyone is ignorant, only on different subjects. —Will Rogers, humorist

The U.S. educational system was designed for the needs of industry during the industrial revolution—to create a mass of people who could read, write and follow instructions. It does not foster the sense of joy that inspires independence, innovative thinking, and creativity. In other words, most people in the United States grew up afraid of making mistakes and embarrassing themselves. But few great achievements have ever been realized without a great many mistakes made in the process.

—Terry Braverman, *Enhance Your Sense of Self-Mirth*, Training and Development

Creativity: Out-of-the-Box Thinking

The phrase, "Out of the Box" is based on the nine-dot box puzzle. Many people are not familiar with that puzzle, so I am including it here. Play with it until you discover the answer. There is a clue to the solution at the beginning of this paragraph.

9-Dot Puzzle

The challenge is to connect all nine dots by drawing four straight lines without having your pen leave the page.

Out-of-the-box thinking is creative thinking, beyond where we would normally go in seeking solutions or new possibilities for our lives. British actor John Cleese, of Monty Python fame, has studied creativity. He asserts that humor is one of the fastest ways to creative thinking.

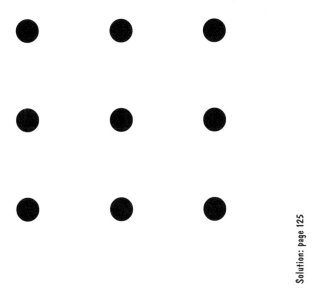

Solution: page 125

There's a window of vulnerability that opens up when people are laughing. They let down their guard and new ideas can come in.
—Kate Clinton, comedian

Author Ekhart Tolle, in his book *The Power of Now*, suggests that increasing our effectiveness in out-of-the-box thinking might involve NOT thinking. He asserts that we are addicted to thinking. The fact that our mind is running all the time may be a hindrance to creativity and spiritual growth rather than a good thing. When we are laughing, we are actually giving our minds a break; perhaps we are even washing our brains.

In studying humor, "incongruity" is a word often identified as the basis of most humor. Synonyms for "incongruous" are "out of place," "incompatible," "inconsistent," "inappropriate," and "odd." Incongruity is a source of humor as well as creativity—putting things together that seem not to belong. It helps us to come up with new ideas and inventions. One inventor, Steven Sample, writes:

When Mark Parisi, the above cartoonist, was born on a New England evening in 1961, the attending physician supposedly mentioned seeing doodles on the uterus wall, but this remains unconfirmed.

I was having trouble designing a new control system for a washing machine. So I forced myself to contemplate outrageous combinations such as how a hay bale or a ladybug or the planet Saturn would handle the job. Of course, nothing useful came directly out of these thoughts—Saturn wasn't going to run a household appliance. But after these strenuous sessions of thinking free, I returned to thinking about the problem from a practical standpoint. Then the answer came quickly—a combination of existing components so simple that I wondered why I hadn't thought of it before. By allowing my mind to explore the question in unusual ways, I unlocked its potential.

Bottom Line Personal

Mark Twain suggests, *"Wit is the marriage between ideas which before their marriage were not perceived to have any relationship."*

Creativity is allowing yourself to make mistakes. Art is knowing which ones to keep.

—Scott Adams, cartoonist

Ideas

What forms of play do you enjoy with others? How do you relax when you are alone? Schedule time to play. With groups I enjoy playing cards and games—indoors and out. When I spend play time alone, I am happy when I have a good book to read, an audio-taped story, or a jigsaw puzzle to put together.

Add more play to your life. Philosopher Eric Hoffer said, *"Whenever you trace the origin of a skill or practice which played a crucial role in the ascent of* [humankind], *we usually reach the realm of play."*

Play is a voluntary activity that is at once invigorating and relaxing, challenging and rewarding, unpredictable yet unthreatening, and above all it is a process we enjoy. Play brings us into the 'present time'; it teaches us flexibility and responsiveness; it encourages creativity and inventiveness.

The New Game Plan for Recovery: Rediscovering the Power of Play by Tobin Quereau and Tom Zimmerman

Group Play: I use icebreakers and energizers to increase the comfort level of workshop participants with groups of fourteen to 400 people. These warm-up activities get people laughing uproariously. Some activities involve throwing stuffed animals to each other or playing a tag game in which running is not allowed. It is amazing how these activities warm participants up for learning.

I introduced group juggle to my mother and elderly aunts and uncles. At the time, I didn't have my bag of stuffed animals for the game. I asked my aunt for some rolls of toilet paper. There were six of us sitting in the living room. I started with one roll of toilet paper, establishing a pattern in which we always threw the "tp" to the same person. After we had the pattern down, I added a second roll, and then a third. Soon we were juggling five or six rolls of toilet paper and laughing our heads off. It is one of my fondest memories. I like to think it is one of their fondest memories as well.

The cork car, one person's idea of play and creativity   Photo by Barbara La Valleur

One of my goals in life is to teach everyone on the planet to play group juggle. So far the number is 893,024. What is a playful, impossible life goal for you?

I have taught group juggle to people from Florida to California to Ireland and Germany, as well as to all ages and occupations: doctors, lawyers, teachers, farm credit folks, administrative assistants, and accountants. Stereotypes make us think that a certain group of people would not want to "let down their hair" and have fun. Some of us may have had bad experiences with icebreakers. What was supposed to be play turned out to be embarrassing or stupid. In my experience, as long as there is an atmosphere of emotional and physical safety and the appropriate context is established, everyone enjoys playing.

There are other ice breaker games for creating a sense of community at family reunions or creating a sense of team in the workplace. Check your local library for books on games. Certain board games bring out laughter: Balderdash, Pictionary, Charades, and Cranium are a few favorites of mine.

I was leading get-acquainted activities for an Elderhostel, a fun educational program for people over fifty-five. An older woman went up to an older man and said, "You look just like my third husband." Flabbergasted, he asked, "Well, how many husbands have you had?" She replied with a gleam in her eyes, "Two."

Other ideas for adding humor to life: Sponsor a humor contest with prizes. One superintendent of a school district holds an end-of-the-school-year humor contest. He invites the teachers and other staff members to submit a description of the funny occurrences throughout the year. The collection could eventually be useful as a fundraiser for the school district.

Gather a list of funny words. Ask others to submit their ideas. What do you think is a funny word? There are the ever-popular "peia" words—"onomatopoeia" and "Cassiopeia." I think "duck" is a funny word. According to Laughlab, the duck is the preferred animal in animal jokes.

Start your own craze like Beanie Babies. See how long it takes to catch on.

Create your own Top 10 list—aka David Letterman. You choose the topic and get your friends together to brainstorm the list. It could help you to lighten up and be more creative about a serious issue.

Audiovisuals are great sources of lightness. Join others in making a funny video about the different forms of humor in your family or at your workplace. A collection of types of laughter can be an ongoing source of humor. Many people make photo albums and scrapbooks of family history. Why not audiotape the family history of funny memories? Audiotape the laughter of the ones you love.

When was the last time you treated yourself to a funny video? Check out some of the humor classics like Charlie Chaplin, the Marx Brothers or Abbott and Costello, Lucille Ball or Carol Burnett. Have a video fest on a snowy or rainy day. Invite people to bring a clip from their favorite funny video.

Humor Tours and Other Occasions for Laughter: Take family and friends on a mystery tour to the local magic store, fun gift shops, or other fun, funny places. Create a magical, mystery tour of your own —looking for the absurdity in everyday life. Create a mystery tour of sites within twenty miles of your own hometown. Wouldn't this be a different approach to a high school reunion?

Create a tour of the absurd in your home, office, apartment building, or neighborhood. When you travel, ask about the fun, unusual places to visit. San Francisco's Science Museum exhibits some of Gary Larson's *Far Side* cartoons. There is a lot of science in many of his cartoons (which may explain why some of us don't get them). Different jokes for different folks.

Have a story telling contest or "jokathon" to raise money for your favorite cause. You might decide to have a panel of judges screen the entries. Give a prize for the person who can tell the most jokes or who laughs the longest. Give awards for the funniest comment of the month or the most creative idea. Sponsor a different contest each month, such as a joke contest, cartoon contest, humorous quotes, quotes about humor, funny objects like mugs and T-shirts, funny bumper sticker contest, and—my favorites—the funny, real life stories that happen at work. Create a point system where everyone gets a vote. Be sure to have great prizes.

Some people think they couldn't remember a joke to save their lives. To remember a joke (only the keepers), give it away within a day. Tell five friends (unless you know someone who will listen five times). Better yet, become a card-carrying humorist. You don't have to rely on your memory for funny things—carry a cartoon or a joke to share with others while standing in lines in restaurants or stores.

Improvised tennis "net"   Photo by Barbara LaValleur

IX

Laugh and Love Yourself
Humility—The Key to Humor

"Worse Than a Clown"

There was a young monk in China who was a very serious practitioner of the Dharma. Once, this monk came across something he did not understand, so he went to ask the master. When the master heard the question, he started laughing. The master then stood up and walked away, still laughing.

The young monk was very disturbed by the master's reaction. For the next three days, he could neither eat, sleep nor think properly. At the end of the three days, he went back to the master and told the master how he felt. When the master heard this, he said, "Monk, do you know what your problem is? Your problem is that YOU ARE WORSE THAN A CLOWN!"

The monk was shocked to hear that, "Venerable Sir, how can you say such a thing?! How can I be worse than a clown?"

The master explained, "A clown enjoys seeing people laugh. You? You feel disturbed because another person laughed. Tell me; are you not worse than a clown?" When the monk heard this, he began to laugh. He was enlightened.

From old Zen records of China

The monk in this story exhibits a lack of humility in his seriousness and is then enlightened and demonstrates humility. No one can laugh at us if we choose to join them.

112

After living fifty-five years and collecting over 110 ways to give and receive humor (the ideas listed in this book with a gray background), I figured out that the key to humor is humility. The ideas, the opportunities for adding lightness to your life, are about doing. Humility is about being. Once again, I see it as an exploration in relational trust.

It is no coincidence that I wrote this book while associating with a Benedictine monastery where humility is recognized as an invaluable virtue. For fourteen centuries the Benedictines have lived according to *The Rule of Benedict*. Benedict recognized that humility was the key to living together in community and developing a relationship with God.

In *The Rule of Benedict: Insights for the Ages*, author and Benedictine Sister Joan Chittister writes that humility is "the foundation for our relationship with God, our connectedness to others, our acceptance of ourselves, our way of using the goods of the earth. . . ." These four themes bring together many concepts already explored in this book, particularly the notion of relational trust. In this case relational trust is not only with others and the God of our understanding, but also with ourselves and the earth.

I first heard of the connection between humor, humility, and being human while facilitating workshops for Hazelden with Ernie Kurtz, co-author of *The Spirituality of Imperfection*. Ernie writes about the importance of embracing our humanity. We are neither beast nor angel, but both beast and angel. When we forget this, we are often hard on ourselves, thinking we should be perfect or more than we are. Other times we get caught thinking we are greater than we are.

In a conversation about the nature of alcoholism, Ernie asked Dr. Dan Anderson, former president of Hazelden, "Do you think the alcoholic's problem is that they think they are special or that they think they are worms?" Dan responded, "Ernie, Ernie, Ernie, the problem is that they think they are 'special worms.'" Alcoholics do not have a corner on the "special worm" market. As human beings, sometimes we think we are special. Other times we think we are worms. Then there are the times we think we are special worms.

No one can make you feel inferior without your consent.
—Eleanor Roosevelt, humanitarian

Some dictionaries associate humility with meekness, modesty, and low rank, words that seem to put us down. Not long ago, it was associated with self-deprecation. To be humble meant to be a doormat. In fact, some of us learned that being humble meant saying negative things about ourselves.

When I was asked to write about my insights on "lessons learned," I was proud—very, very proud. In fact, as an old Lutheran, I was beginning to think that I was thinking more highly of myself than I ought. But then I remembered the words of that old Lutheran hymn: "For I am weak and weary, and sinful and defiled." And I felt so much better.

—Merrilyn Belgum, comedian

The understanding of humility is taking on a more positive tone. It is accepting ourselves as we are and as we are not. It is about integrity, accepting ourselves as whole and complete and, at the same time, still in process. It is a paradox—to be complete and to be continuing to develop as human beings. Humility is about gratitude and appreciation of who we are, who others are, and who God is. It is about owning and celebrating our gifts, recognizing them as gifts—contributing our gifts to the whole.

I'm good enough, smart enough, and doggone it, people like me.

—Stuart Smalley (really Al Franken)

The Truth about Myself

O God,
Help me to believe
The truth about myself—
No matter how beautiful it is!

—Macrina Wiederkehr, O.S.B.
From *WomanPrayer* by Mary Ford-Grabowsky

Healthy Laughing at Ourselves vs. Self-deprecation

You grow up the day you have your first real laugh at yourself.

—Ethel Barrymore, entertainer

Obviously, I am a fervent proponent of lightheartedness. It is vital to lighten up—to appreciate the funny aspects of our humanity. One of the crucial lessons is learning to distinguish healthy laughing at ourselves from caustic self-deprecation. The key to this distinction is accepting ourselves, making a conscious choice to laugh at ourselves and let others in on the joke. Part of the choice has to do with confidence, having a certain amount of healthy self-esteem and self-acceptance.

In *Clowning in Rome*, theologian Henri Nouwen tells the story of a friend who gave him a photograph of a water lily. When asked how he produced such a splendid picture, his friend replied, "Well, I had to be very patient and very attentive. It was only after a few hours of compliments that the lily was willing to let me take her picture."

Some of us learned to make fun of ourselves as a defense mechanism with self-deprecating humor as a shield. We ridiculed ourselves before anyone else could. Comedian Carol Burnett describes her experience:

I subconsciously decided to hit myself first before anyone else did. I'll put down my figure. I'll put down my face. I'll do the flat-chested jokes. The kind of humor that was acceptable for a woman was being man-crazy and putting yourself down. I wanted to strike first so nobody else would. That was before the feminist movement took hold, and now, I would never do that.

Laughing at ourselves in public, however, can be a conscious choice, a tool to put others at ease. *Look Who's Laughing* is a video about comedians with disabilities discussing their deliberate choice to use their disability or not as a source of humor to increase the comfort of the audience.

115

For example, Geri Jewell, a comedian with cerebral palsy, quips: "The worst thing about having CP is trying to pluck my eyebrows. How do you think I got pierced ears?"

In *Queens of Comedy*, Susan Horowitz describes an incident when Geri Jewell attended a taping of *The Carol Burnett Show*. "She feigned deafness to get a front row seat. Carried away, she waved her hand for attention. When Burnett called on her, the usher explained that Jewell was deaf. 'No, I'm not!' she blurted out. As the audience stared, Jewell gulped, and then cried out with religious fervor, 'Oh my God! I can hear!'"

Recently I was able to laugh at myself and my lack of organization. A few months ago I won a twenty-dollar gift certificate. I used it as a bookmark in the book I was reading at the time. When I picked the book up several weeks later, there it was. I was a winner for the second time. Thankfully the certificate had not expired. According to the creator of Winnie the Pooh, A.A. Milne, *"One of the advantages of being disorderly is that one is constantly making exciting discoveries."*

From *Children's Letters to God*:
> *Dear GOD,*
> *I am doing the best I can. Really.   Frank.*

Once again humor is a diagnostic tool. When we are lacking humor, it is time to check our level of confidence, self-esteem, and humility. Self-criticism and harsh judgment interfere with humor. The Constant Commentator on our shoulder is often our worst critic. To counter the constant critic whispering in our ears, give the voice a name—such as Niggling Nasty Nellie. Whatever you do, don't argue with her. That just gives her more attention. Thank her for sharing and move on. Or say to yourself, "Cancel, cancel."

Learning to accept ourselves as we are is a lifelong process.

What if the question is not why am I so infrequently the person I want to be, but why do I so infrequently want to be the person I am?
—Oriah Mountain Dreamer, author

While writing this book, I often expected myself to be the perfect thinker and writer. The words should just flow out of my head or heart through my fingertips to the keys of the keyboard, and onto the printed page with ease. Actually the words did flow, not necessarily in the right order. It made a difference to be able to laugh at my expectations, at my lack of self-acceptance. "Shoulding" on ourselves is a sure sign that humor and humility are missing.

I shouldn't *should* on myself or anyone else.

—Linda Hutchinson, *ha!*

At one point when I was frustrated that this book was not coming together as fast as I thought it should (there I go again), I realized that even though I wasn't perfect, I was making progress. Thirty years ago, a professor friend teased me about not finishing my sentences. Today I finish sentences. I am even learning to finish paragraphs.

I'm writing a book. I've got the page numbers done.

—Steven Wright, comedian

At another point in the process, my friend Paul told me that my "voice" was missing from the manuscript. Imagine that—writing a book without a voice. I realized I was allowing my tendency to avoid controversy to take over. Since humor is a controversial subject, I was operating from my fear and not from my commitment to communicate the power and possibility of humor. When I attempt to please everyone, I sell out on myself. I was given a T-shirt with the slogan: **You are entitled to my opinion.** As I lightened up, I gained courage to express my opinion.

Parable: A boy rode on the donkey while an old man walked. As they went along, some people remarked, "It is a shame the old man is walking and the boy is riding." The man and boy thought maybe the critics were right, so they changed positions. Later, they passed some people that remarked, "What a shame. He makes that little boy walk." They decided they both would walk! Soon they passed some more people who thought they were stupid to walk when they had a decent donkey to ride. So they both

rode the donkey! Now they passed some people that shamed them saying, "How awful to put such a load on a poor donkey." The boy and man said they were probably right, so they decided to carry the donkey. As they crossed a bridge, they lost their grip on the donkey, and it fell into the river and drowned. The Moral of the Story: If you try to please everyone, you will eventually lose your ass.

Perhaps lack of humility is about fear. It is possible to transform fear with laughter. The answer to fear is love, laughter and humility. We all want to look good. Our attempts at looking good can be a great source of humor.

Real freedom comes from unabashedly being oneself despite what others think.
—Andrew Harvey, author

Humility is not only about accepting ourselves; it is also about creating who we are, having the courage to be authentic. The root word for "authentic" is "auctor," which I interpret as being the "author of our lives."

Statesman Dag Hammarskjold said:

Humility is just as much the opposite of self-abasement as it is of self-exultation. To be humble is not to make comparisons. Secure in its reality, the self is neither better nor worse, bigger nor smaller, than anything else in the universe. It is—nothing, yet at the same time one with everything.

Did you hear the one about the yogi ordering a hot dog at the hot dog stand? He said, "Make me one with everything."

Hum'rous
Live life freely
Laugh at one's own antics
Muse at life's incongruities
Humble?
—Sister Janet Thielges, O.S.B.

About Connecting with Others

My name used to be Me. But now it's You.
—Theophane the Monk

According to the dictionary, humility is the feeling or attitude that you have no special importance that makes you better than others. Humor can be a means to connect or to separate and distance ourselves from others.

It is my belief that those of us with privileges based on our gender, race, class, education, and other forms of status, are to use the privileges to connect with others. One way to do this is through humor. The ability to laugh at ourselves with others levels the playing field especially with those who have fewer privileges.

Consider how to use humor as a contribution and means to create a greater sense of belonging, especially among those who feel left out.

**Those who get too big for their britches
will be exposed in the end.**

On 2,760 Web sites

From Anne Cameron, *Daughters of Copper Woman*, "We needed our clowns, and we used 'em to help us learn the best ways to get along with each other. Bein' an individual is real good, but sometimes we're so busy bein' individuals we forget we gotta live with a lot of people who all got the right to be individuals, too, and the clowns could show us if we were getting a bit pushy, or startin' to take ourselves too seriously."

Philosopher Bertrand Russell said that one of the symptoms of approaching a nervous breakdown is a belief that one's work is terribly important.

The humble person has the courage to be imperfect. While working at Hazelden, my job included coaching presenters for professional educational workshops to deliver their. One woman gave a presentation on Quality Assurance. Of course, she wanted not only to be top quality, but perfect. I reassured her that she would make a mistake, to be ready for it, and to use it as a means to relate with the participants. Participants are more open to learning from someone who is not "above" them. Learners need to be able to identify with their teacher.

Turn mistakes into opportunities for humor. Invariably when I am in front of people writing on a flip chart, even though I was a spelling bee champion, the correct spelling of words disappears. I've learned to blame it on the magic marker, or to ask: "When will they make markers that do spell check?" Doing this increases the comfort level of the participants and of me. When we get puffed up about ourselves, often there are opportunities to be brought back down to earth.

The connection between humor and humility is shown when we attempt to play God and the rug is pulled out from under us or we slip on a banana peel, literally or figuratively. Humor can be our saving grace. What does St. Paul say, pride goeth before the fall? Humor is a wonderful way to embrace our humanity. *Humor reduces problems and people to their proper proportions.* (Author unknown)

Time between slipping on a banana peel and smacking the pavement equals one bananosecond.

That reminds me of the story of a minister who wrote a sermon on humility, then filed it away for a really big occasion when he could impress a lot of people.

In *Spirituality and Comedy*, Conrad Hyers describes the mature sense of humor as based on acceptance and inner harmony: "It presupposes faith in some sacred order or depth-dimension of being, some common basis of worth and dignity while at the same time refusing to dogmatize its understanding of faith and worth." It is capable of becoming a humor of love and mercy.

Hyers describes various levels of humor, beginning with the playful innocence of childhood. The next, or adolescent level, focuses on truth and justice. It is a time of judging the follies and hypocrisies of others and discharging tension. The mature sense of humor based on humility and compassion dispenses good will and a kind of divine grace.

In a *Parabola* magazine issue on humor, theologian Helen Luke asserts that the capacity to appreciate and understand characterizes the mature sense of humor. She suggests that the wisdom and compassion of the understanding heart is indeed the core of the laughter that is born from the mature sense of humor.

Humus: Relationship with the Earth

My friend Sister Sheila Rausch, O.S.B., says, "Humor and humility are inextricably related. . . . The two converge in their relationship to *humus*, ground. Humility requires knowing one's earthly origin. Result? One finds human behavior, circumstances and events often amusing or comical. Why? Because of the stark contrast between one's aspirations and destiny—sublime and even divine—and the facts of human life. Being able to laugh at oneself renders life hilarious."

I asked Sister Sheila for an example from her life. She wrote, "Although I never seriously envisioned a career in acting, I did take part in amateur dramatics in college. And as the youngest of two in my family, I developed performance to a high art. I could and did 'get my way' by feigning heartbreak and producing real sobs and tears. Some years ago I outgrew such shameless artifice. Even today, however, as I celebrate seventy-seven years on this earth, I am capable of apparently contradictory behavior. Even on a cold day (if not below forty degrees and without much wind), I thoroughly enjoy a brisk bike ride. On the other hand, if there is heavy work to be done—especially if it involves lifting, bending below the waist, or picking anything off the floor—I will effortlessly don a pained expression to discourage any onlookers from asking me to help. If necessary I may remind them that while I would just love to be helpful, the fact is that I am only a shriveled specimen sitting around waiting for knee surgery."

Humus, humor, and humility are about accepting our humanity—loving ourselves and each other as we are and as we are not. It is about knowing our place in the Grand Scheme. Perhaps the link between the words "humor" and "humus" is to remind us that we are dust and unto dust we shall return. Another friend, Sister Pauline Fernandes, posts a reminder on her door: *"Don't take life too seriously. It is only a temporary arrangement."*

**If you can't laugh at yourself,
you really are missing the best joke in town.**

Final HQ Test
Your Humor Quotient

Directions: Read aloud to yourself or to another person. It's funnier that way.

1.	People tell me one thing one day and out the other.	True	False
2.	I can't unclasp my hands.	True	False
3.	I can wear my shirt as pants.	True	False
4.	I feel as much like I did yesterday as I do today.	True	False
5.	I frequently lick the front of postage stamps.	True	False
6.	I occasionally mistake my hands for food.	True	False
7.	I'd rather eat soap than little stones.	True	False
8.	I never liked room temperature.	True	False
9.	My throat is closer than it seems.	True	False
10.	I'm being followed by boxer shorts.	True	False
11.	Most things are better eaten than forgotten.	True	False
12.	Likes and dislikes are among my favorite things.	True	False
13.	Pudding without raisins is no pudding at all.	True	False
14.	I've lost all sensation in my shirt.	True	False
15.	I've always known when to close my eyes.	True	False
16.	My squirrels don't know where I am tonight.	True	False
17.	Walls impede my progress.	True	False
18.	I can't find all my marmots.	True	False
19.	There's only one thing for me.	True	False
20.	My uncle is as stupid as paste.	True	False
21.	I can pet animals by the mouthful.	True	False
22.	My toes are numbered.	True	False
23.	A person's reach should exceed his overbite.	True	False
24.	I can find my ears, but I have to look.	True	False
25.	I don't like any of my loved ones.	True	False

If you checked *true* in fewer than 5 instances, reread this book.

If you checked *true* in 5 to 9 instances, your sense of humor needs a transfusion.

If you checked *true* in 10 to 14 instances, I know where your marmots are.

If you checked *true* in 15 to 19 instances, your sense of humor is doing well.

If you checked *true* in 20 to 25 instances, I know a good therapist.

A selection from R.R. Vallacher, C. Gilbert, and D.M. Wegner's
Hidden Brain Damage Scale, *American Psychologist*

Afterword

Riddle:
Five frogs sitting on a log.
One decided to jump off.
How many frogs are sitting on the log?

The answer is not 4. The clue is in the second line.

A decision to act is not the same as action, so the number of frogs hasn't changed. What will you take on to add more humor to your life? Schedule the action on your calendar. Get a humor buddy to support you.

Solution to puzzle on page 105.

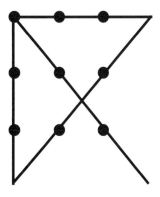

Bibliography

Books

Ayre, Leslie. *The Wit of Music.* Boston: Crescendo Publishing Company, 1966.

Barreca, Regina. *They Used to Call Me Snow White—But I Drifted: Women's Strategic Use of Humor.* New York: Viking, 1991.

Benard, Cheryl. *Veiled Courage: Inside the Afghan Women's Resistance.* New York: Broadway Books, 2002.

Berger, Peter L. *Redeeming Laughter: the Comic Dimension of Human Experience.* New York: Walter de Gruyter, 1997.

Blumenfeld, Esther and Lynn Alperne. *Humor at Work: The Guaranteed, Bottom-Line, Low-Cost, High-Efficiency Guide to Success through Humor.* Atlanta, Georgia: Peachtree Publishers, 1994.

British Association for the Advancement of Science. *Laughlab: The Scientific Quest for the World's Funniest Joke.* London: Arrow Books Ltd. Random House Group, 2002.

Broden, Sarita. "Therapeutic Use of Humor in the Treatment of Eating Disorders; Or, There Is Life Even after Fat Thighs." *Eating Disorders: New Directions in Treatment and Recovery.* New York: Columbia University Press, 1994.

Burgess, Ron. *Laughing Lessons: 149 ½ Ways to Make Teaching and Learning Fun.* Minneapolis: Free Spirit Publishing, 2000.

Cameron, Anne. *Daughters of Copper Woman.* Vancouver, BC: Press Gang Publishers, 1981.

Chittister, Joan, OSB. *The Rule of Benedict: Insights for the Ages.* New York: Crossroad, 1992.

Clinton, Kate. *Don't Get Me Started.* Random House, 1998.

Conn, Joann Wolski, ed. *Women's Spirituality: Resources for Christian Development.* New York: Paulist Press, 1986.

Cousins, Norman. *Anatomy of an Illness as Perceived by the Patient: Reflections on Healing and Regeneration.* New York: Norton, 1979.

Crum, Thomas. *The Magic of Conflict: Turning a Life of Work into a Work of Art.* New York: Touchstone, 1987.

Curran, Dolores. *Traits of a Healthy Family: Fifteen Traits Commonly Found in - Healthy Families by Those Who Work with Them.* Minneapolis: Winston Press, 1983.

Dance, Daryl Cumber. *Honey Hush!: An Anthology of African American Women's Humor.* New York: W.W. Norton, 1998.

Deloria, Vine. "Indian Humor." *Race, Class, and Gender: an Anthology.* Belmont, California: Wadsworth, 2001.

De Mello, Anthony. *Awakening: Conversations with the Master.* Chicago: Loyola Press, 1998.

De Mello, Anthony. *Writings/Selected with an Introduction by William Dych.* Maryknoll, New York: Orbis Books, 1999.

Elffers, Joost. *Play with Your Food.* New York: Stewart, Tabori & Change, 1997.

Farzan, Massud. *Another Way of Laughter: A Collection of Sufi Humor.* New York: Dutton, 1973.

Feigelson, Sheila. *Energize Your Meetings with Laughter.* Alexandria, Virginia: Association for Supervision and Curriculum Development, 1998.

Ford-Grabowsky, Mary. *WomanPrayers: Prayers by Women Throughout History and Around the World.* San Francisco: HarperSanFrancisco, 2003.

Goodman, Joel. *Laffirmations.* Deerfield Beach, Florida: Health Communications, 1995.

Goss, Tracy. *The Last Word on Power: Re-invention for Leaders and Anyone Who Must Make the Impossible Happen.* New York: Currency Doubleday, 1996.

Gregory, Dick. *Nigger.* New York: Simon and Schuster, 1964.

Hample, Stuart (Compiler), Eric Marshall (Introduction), and Tom Bloom (Illustrator). *Children's Letters to God.* New York: Workman Publishing Company, 1991.

Hart, Hilary. *The Unknown She: Eight Faces of an Emerging Consciousness.* Inverness, California: Golden Sufi Center, 2003.

Hollander, Nicole. *Ma, Can I Be a Feminist and Still Like Men?* New York: St. Martin's Press, 1980.

Hollander, Nicole. *Hi, This is Sylvia. I Can't Come to the Phone Right Now, So When You Hear the Beep, Please Hang Up.* New York: St. Martin's Press, 1983.

Horowitz, Susan. *Queens of Comedy: Lucille Ball, Phyllis Diller, Carol Burnett, Joan Rivers, and the New Generation of Funny Women.* Australia: Gordon and Breach Publishers, 1997.

Kataria, Madan. *Laughter for No Reason.* Andheri (W), Mumbai, India: Madhuri International, 1999.

Kaufman, Gloria, ed. *In Stitches: a Patchwork of Feminist Humor and Satire.* Bloomington: Indiana University Press, 1991.

Kaufman, Goria, and Mary Kay Blakely, eds. *Pulling Our Own Strings: Feminist Humor and Satire.* Bloomington: Indiana University Press, 1980.

Keough, William. *Punchlines: The Violence of American Humor.* New York: Paragon House, 1990.

Klein, Allen. *The Courage to Laugh: Humor, Hope, and Healing in the Face of Death and Dying.* New York: J.P. Tarcher/Putnam, 1998.

Klein, Allen. *The Healing Power of Humor.* New York: J.P. Tarcher/Putnam, 1989.

Kurtz, Ernest and Katherine Ketcham. *The Spirituality of Imperfection: Modern Wisdom from Classic Stories.* New York: Bantam Books, 1992.

LaRoche, Loretta. *Relax—You May Only Have a Few Minutes Left.* New York: Villard, 1998.

La Roche, Loretta. *Life Is Not a Stress Rehearsal: Bringing Yesterday's Sane Wisdom into Today's Insane World.* New York: Broadway Books, 2001.

Lundin, Stephen C. and others. *Fish! Tales.* New York: Hyperion Books, 2002.

Nouwen, Henri J.M. *Clowning in Rome: Reflections on Solitude, Celibacy, Prayer and*

Bibliography

Contemplation. Garden City, New York: Image Books, 1979.

Metcalf, C.W. and Roma Felible. *Lighten Up: Survival Skills for People under Pressure.* Reading, Massachusetts: Addison Wesley Publishing Co., 1992.

Petras, Ross and Kathryn Petras. *776 Stupidest Things Ever Said.* Main Street Books, Doubleday, 1993.

Quereau, Tobin and Tom Zimmerman. *The New Game Plan for Recovery: Rediscovering the Power of Play.* Ballantine Books, 1992.

Rilke, Rainer Maria. *Letters to a Young Poet.* New York: Random House, 1984.

Robinson, Vera M. *Humor and the Health Professions : the Therapeutic Use of Humor in Health Care.* Thorofare, New Jersey: Slack Inc., 1991.

Romano, Ray, Everything and a Kite. Bantam, 1998.

Shannon, William H. *"Something of a Rebel" Thomas Merton His Life and Works: An Introduction.* Cincinnatti: St. Anthony Messenger Press, 1997.

Sochen, June. *Women's Comic Visions.* Detroit: Wayne State University Press, 1991.

Stetz, Margaret D. *British Women's Comic Fiction, 1890-1990: Not Drowning, But Laughing.* Burlington, Vermont: Ashgate, 2001.

Tillemans, Rose. *Savoring Grace: A Year at Peace House.* Winona, Minnesota: St. Mary's Press, 1997.

Tillemans, Rose. *I'm Still Dancing: Praying through Good Days and Bad.* Mystic, Connecticut: Twenty-third Publications, 2003.

Timmerman, Joan H. *The Mardi Gras Syndrome: Rethinking Christian Sexuality.* New York: Crossroad Publishing Company, 1984.

Timmerman, Joan H. *Sexuality and Spiritual Growth.* New York: Crossroad Publishing Company, 1992.

Tolle, Eckhart. *The Power of Now.* Novato, California: New World Library, 1999.

Travis, Cheryl Brown and Jacquelyn W. White, eds. *Sexuality, Society, and Feminism.* Washington, D.C.: American Psychological Association, 2000.

Twist, Lynne. *The Soul of Money.* New York: W.W. Norton, 2003.

Van Dyke, Dick. *Faith, Hope and Hilarity.* Garden City, New York: Doubleday, 1971.

Vass, Susan. *Laughing Your Way to Good Health.* HMR Publications Group, Inc., 1989.

Wagner, Jane. *The Search for Signs of Intelligent Life in the Universe.* New York: Harper & Row, 1986.

Walker, Alice. *The Color Purple.* New York: Harcourt Brace Jovanovich, 1982.

Walker, Nancy and Zita Dresner. *Redressing the Balance: American Women's Literary Humor from Colonial Times to the 1980s.* Jackson: University Press of Mississippi, 1988.

Warren, Roz, ed. *Revolutionary Laughter.* Berkeley, California: Crossing Press, 1995.

Wasserman, Miriam and Linda Hutchinson, *Teaching Human Dignity: Social Change Lessons for Everyteacher.* Minneapolis: Education Exploration Center, 1978.

Zander, Rosamund Stone and Benjamin Zander. *The Art of Possibility: Transforming Professional and Personal Life.* Boston: Harvard Business School Press, 2000.

Web Sites

www.ashleighbrilliant.com>

www.dharmathecat.com>

www.gohmongboy.com>

www.haha-team.com>

www.landmarkeducation.com
www.laughlab.com>
www.lorettalaroche.com>
www.thehumorproject.com>
www.soulofmoney.org
www.wakeuplaughing.com/index.shtml>.
www.worldlaughtertour.com>

Videos

Buckley, Kathy, J.D. England, Brett Leake, Chris Fonseca, Alex Valex and Geri Jewell. *Look Who's Laughing.* Program Development Associates, 1994.
Goodheart, Annette. *The Art of Laughter Therapy.* Santa Barbara, California: Goodheart, Inc., 1990.

Articles/Magazines

Bottom Line Personal, March 15, 2002, Vol 23, #6. www.BottomLine Secrets.com1.
Braverman, Terry. "Enhance Your Sense of Self-Mirth." *Training and Development*, July 1993.
Heffner, David. "Spirit in a World of Connection." *National Catholic Reporter*, May 2, 2003.
Luke, Helen. "The Laughter at the Heart of Things." *Parabola*. Winter 1987, XII, 4.
Mitlan, Jessica. "Make Protests Fun: 1-2-3-4, we don't want shrill chants no more." *Utne Reader,* March-April 2003.
Utne, Nina. "Think Pink." *Utne Reader*, March-April 2003.
"Vallacher, R.R., Gilbert, C., and Wegner, D.M., "The Hidden Brain Damage Scale." *American Psychologist*, 1979, 33, 192.

Miscellaneous

DiSC Personal Profiles. Inscape Publishing. Distributed by Hutchinson Associates, *ha!* www.haha-team.com.

Linda Hutchinson is an adult educator, author, and owner of Hutchinson Associates, *ha!* She and her associates design and deliver training programs and keynote addresses for large and small corporations, non-profit organizations, and professional associations. Topics besides humor include team building, leadership, diversity, customer service, and stress and time management.

Linda, who has a Masters of Arts and Theology, leads retreats on humor and spirituality and teaches a college course on sexuality and spiritual growth at The College of St. Catherine, St. Paul, Minnesota.

Linda's real claim to fame is that she was a contestant on *Bowling for Dollars*! She got a spare and won ten dollars.

www.haha-team.com